Never To Return

(Convoys to Russia in the Second World War)

by

Roderick G Maclean

POINTMEDIA

Never To Return

(Convoys to Russia in the Second World War)

by Roderick G Maclean

Design by Jane Cornwell

ISBN: 978–1–0369–0326–8

PointMedia Ltd
Isle of Lewis
www.pointmedia.tv

About the Author, Roderick G Maclean

Roderick G Maclean was born in Ibrox, Glasgow in 1954, and he grew up in a family which conversed in Gaelic every day. His parents were from the Isle of Skye. Roderick and his wife, Morag, have lived and worked in the Isle of Lewis for almost 40 years. In that time, he has been a lecturer at Lews Castle College, Gaelic Museums Education Officer for Museum nan Eilean, and Depute Rector of The Nicolson Institute. He was awarded a PhD in 1994 by the University of Glasgow for research he carried out on immersion courses in Israel.

When Roderick was growing up in Glasgow in the 1960s, his mother would say to him on New Year's Eve: 'David was lost on the Russian convoys.' That was all. There was no more information to give because the family had none. David Macdonald, her first cousin from Waternish, Skye went down with HMS *Achates* on Thursday 31 December, 1942. He was 22 years of age. David's niece, and namesake, Davina Matthews was born a number of months after the loss of the *Achates*. For more than 60 years she had been looking for details concerning David's death, but without success. In 2012, following a chance discussion on the topic, her quest motivated Roderick, her cousin, to begin researching the *Achates'* story and by a set of fortuitous links he discovered the final moments of David's life. This book tells the story of the Arctic Convoys and the bravery of the naval personnel in the Battle of the Barents Sea on that last day of 1942.

On 11 September 1928, the keel of HMS *Achates* (H12) was laid at John Brown's shipyard on the River Clyde

On 31 December 1942, the keel of HMS *Achates* (H12) was sunk in the Arctic Ocean by the Kriegsmarine

This is a story about the convoys to Russia, the heroes who sailed on them, and the destroyer HMS *Achates*

Contents

Upon this battle depends the
  survival of Christian civilization.

Upon it depends our own British life
  and the long continuity of our
    institutions, and our Empire.

The whole fury and might of the enemy
  must very soon be turned on us.

Hitler knows that we will hv to break
  us in this Island, or lose the war.

If we can stand up to him,
      all Europe may be freed,
        and the life of the world
          may move forward into the
            broad and sunlit uplands.

But if we fail,
    then the whole world,
      including the United States,
        and all that we have known and
                              cared for,
          will sink into the abyss of a
            new Dark Age
                made more sinister and
                  perhaps more prolonged by
                    the lights of perverted
                              Science.

Let us therefore brace ourselves to
    our duty, and so bear ourselves that
      if the British Empire and
        Commonwealth lasts for a
          thousand years, men will still
            say,

    'This was their finest hour'.

Churchill's 'Finest Hour' speech notes

CHAPTER 1

THE TREACHERY OF WAR

During the Second World War between 1940 and 1941, Britain suffered terribly and came close to losing its struggle against the Nazis. Were it not that 338,000 soldiers, one third of them French, had been miraculously ferried back to Britain within the space of eight days, the country would have been deprived of its only trained fighting force. The successful implementation of Operation Dynamo saved the Allied cause from collapse and created the famous 'Dunkirk spirit' which permeated Britain and inspired continued defiance against Hitler and his armed forces through the summer of 1940 and beyond.

Operation Dynamo had begun on 27 May, 1940 and had ended at 09:30 on the morning of 4 June. Just over a fortnight later, at 6:30pm in the evening of Saturday 22 June, France signed a surrender agreement. Hitler demanded that the signing be carried out in the same railway carriage and at the same location as the French commander-in-chief, Ferdinand Foch, had made Germany sign armistice terms at 11:00 am on November 11, 1918, to end the First World War. Many Germans, and historians, considered that the later terms imposed upon Germany in the Treaty of Versailles (signed June 28, 1919) were overly punitive and unjust. In revenge, Hitler commanded Foch's railway carriage be removed from a French museum and relocated to the city of Compiègne, about 50 miles north of Paris for the signing.

Britain was now alone against Germany and Prime Minister Churchill knew the situation was critical. The gravity of his speech in the House of Commons on 18 June, 1940 still resonates:

... What General Weygand has called the Battle of France is over. I expect the Battle of Britain is about to begin. Upon this battle depends the survival of

Christian civilisation. Upon it depends our own British life, and the long continuity of our institutions and our Empire...

Let us therefore brace ourselves to our duty and so bear ourselves that if the British Empire and its Commonwealth lasts for a thousand years, men will still say, 'this was their finest hour'.[1]

One year after France's fall, Hitler commenced Operation Barbarossa.[2] The plan was named after the Holy Roman Emperor Frederick Barbarossa (1152-90) who sought to impose the might of Germany on Europe in the 12th century. Eight centuries later, Hitler and his Nazis sought to impose their might on Stalin's Russia. Barbarossa was a multi-layered stratagem which would begin with the invasion of Russia and culminate in the elimination of over 30 million Slavs. Their territories would be governed by German administrators who would eventually repopulate the area with Aryans, namely, 'pure-blooded' persons of German stock. The plan's purpose was to gain *Lebensraum* (Living Space) for the *Vaterland* (Fatherland), a desire which had existed in Germany since the 1890s. Hitler invaded Russia on Sunday 22 June 1941.

Victory in Russia would give Germany abundant resources. In the Caucasus there were riches of oil, and elsewhere a profusion of fertile farmland. The German nation anticipated reaping these promised riches. If the Slavic captives became unprofitable, they would be executed in accordance with Generalplan Ost (General Plan East). Its objective was to exile the majority of the inhabitants of Middle and Eastern Europe. By 'exile' the Nazis meant removal to Siberia, enslavement, or execution. Generalplan Ost would affect Poles, Ukrainians, Russians, Czechs, and other non-Aryan Slavic nations. German citizens would replace the Slavs and Generalplan Ost would leave its victims to perish through starvation. The food which the Slavs had grown would be transported to Germany to feed the master race.

At the commencement of Operation Barbarossa, 3,000,000 German soldiers invaded Russia along a front which stretched 2,900km (1,800 miles). This was a huge invasion force – the D-Day landings in Normandy comprised 156,000 Allied soldiers. Accompanying the German infantry were around 3,000 tanks, 7,000 artillery guns, and 2,500 planes. Finnish and Romanian units fought with the German troops.

Russia fought ferociously against the Nazis, but required assistance. In 1941, Stalin sought help from Britain, despite Russia initially having been on Germany's side – that is, until Hitler betrayed Stalin through Operation Barbarossa. Churchill's philosophy was to keep Germany fighting on two fronts in order to weaken the Nazi monster. Initially, Stalin wanted the RAF to attack two towns in northern Scandinavia, Kirkenes in Norway and Petsamo in

Finland. The Luftwaffe was using the captured runways in these cities to launch attacks against the Russians. On 30 July, 1941 planes from the Fleet Air Arm (FAA) took off from the decks of HMS *Victorious* and HMS *Furious* as part of Operation EF. Their mission was to bomb the Norwegian and Finnish airfields.

Although Admiral Tovey, Commander of the Home Fleet, had serious reservations about the effectiveness of the plan, the War Cabinet at the Admiralty were adamant that there should be an attack. Tovey knew that at that time of the year there would be no night so far north and, therefore, no cover of darkness. The 'midnight sun' would make a surprise attack impossible. In his opinion, British forces would be in grave danger. Tovey was correct. Nine service personnel were killed and 27 were wounded. Sixteen aircraft were lost without any visible gain from the undertaking. One author described it as an 'unqualified disaster.'[3]

The destroyer, HMS *Achates*, was to form part of the defensive screen for the two aircraft carriers *Victorious* and *Furious*. However, on 25 July 1941, five days before the attack, as the vessels gathered off the coast of Iceland, at 03:00 HMS *Achates* collided with a mine and her bow was ripped open. Worse still, 65 crew who had been in their sleeping quarters in the forward area lost their lives.

One seaman was especially fortunate. Harry Relf was on watch that night and at midnight, following a four hour shift, he went down to the forward sleeping quarters, anticipating some welcome sleep. On arriving, he discovered that the young seaman who was to take his place was suffering badly from seasickness. Harry took pity on him, as this was the young lad's first voyage. Harry said that he would go back on watch for the next four hours. Three hours into the watch, the mine detonated and the young sailor was killed as he slept. Harry Relf, however, was unharmed.[4]

Ronald Weyman was a navigator on the *Achates* at the time and this is how he described events:

Lieutenant Commander
Ronald C Weyman

> *The Captain appeared beside me, scratching his straggly beard. He peered over my shoulder at the chart.*
> *"What do you think, Wey?" He said.*
> *"According to the Admiral's calculations at noon, sir, he says we are here," I replied, indicating a pencilled position on the chart,*

near the east coast of Iceland. "Present course and speed is calculated to bring us close to the minefield at 03:00. We are to skirt the minefield here," I shifted the pencil to a point along our projected course... I descended from the bridge, and made my way in the dark through the familiar orderly clutter of the upper deck.

The steel door creaked under my hand. I closed it and switched on the light. My little cabin was a haven in which the ever-present roar of the sea and the buffeting of the wind were reduced to a murmur... I brushed my teeth, climbed into my bunk, switched off the light and the radio, and to the gentle movement of the sea and the subdued throb of the engines, I fell asleep.

It seemed moments later there was a vast explosion. I was flung out of my bunk, moving so swiftly that my beautiful radio-gramophone, dislodged by the impact, fell on my bunk where a second before my head had rested.

I was already in my clothes, lacking only sea-boots. Around my chest, deflated, was the inseparable Mae West. I thrust my feet into the boots, pulled on my cap, and made for the door. The ship was curiously quiet. The engines had stopped, the deck under my feet was slanting in a peculiar manner. The heavy latch on the door was stiff, and in the dark I wrestled with it. It gave under my effort, and I burst out only to recoil with shock. Virtually everything forward of my cabin – the entire forecastle – had disappeared. Before me there was empty vertiginous space.

Below me, the sea humped, dark and oil-slicked. From a ripped and ragged piece of shattered bulkhead fluttered the remnants of a hammock, torn and bloody. There was an acrid smell of burnt cordite in the air. Strangely, I was alone.

I turned and in the darkness picked my way to the wheelhouse, the deck slanting under my feet. Cole-Hamilton, who had taken over from me earlier, as officer of the watch, was struggling with the ship's wheel. At his feet lay the helmsman, unconscious, bleeding from the mouth.

"See the Captain on the Bridge," said Cole-Hamilton.

I went up top. The Captain was speaking with quiet authority into the engine-room voice-pipe. The crisp voice of our Welsh engineer officer came back reassuringly.

I glanced around the dark horizon. It was empty... The Chief Engineer appeared. He was covered with oil, wiping his hands on a piece of cotton waste. "I can give you two knots, Captain. Going astern."

"Very good, Chief," said [Captain] Jaylen... Jaylen had turned to the chart table. "Number One. We'll head for Swedesford. Thank God for a calm sea." He straightened up, "and let me know the casualties, will you?" "The medical officer's onto it, sir."

"Very good." He turned to me. "We must reduce top-weight, Wey. Would you get a party onto B gundeck and jettison everything you can?"

"Aye, aye, sir."

The Chief had gone back to his engine room, and presently the screws began to thump again under the ship's stern. The broken vessel shuddered throughout her reduced length, and presently began to move going slowly astern, meeting the cold, northern Atlantic waters.

Everything forward of "B" gun-deck was gone. The entire fo'c'sle, "A" gun, mess decks, accommodation for half the ship's company who were asleep at the time of the explosion. All gone. On "B" gun-deck itself, the explosion had caused a shambles. "A" steel gun-shield remained, but it was bent up at a ninety-degree

The mine damage to the bow of HMS *Achates*

angle. Cables and live shells were littered on the tilting wet surface of the deck, along with a greasy substance which made footing precarious.

Some of the ready-use ammunition for the 4.7 had been damaged by the explosion, and now, wet with rain, it was exuding cordite, sending up nauseous fumes.

In that dim growing light of dawn, I collected half a dozen of a work crew – a petty officer, a steward still in his white mess jacket, and together with hacksaws and wrenches and bare hands we did our best to lighten the ship, flinging overboard the bubbling canisters of explosive, lethal 4.7 ammunition, unshackling broken wires and cables, dispensing with whatever we could move. "Wot 'appened, sir?"

"Minefield." [5]

Survivors from the mine explosion

The *Achates* continued astern to Seidisfjord in Iceland to examine the damage. The Admiralty concluded that she could be repaired and returned to service. *Achates* was made watertight and on 7 August the tug *Assurance* towed her back to Britain, with HMS *Anthony* in attendance. On the journey, a storm arose which re-opened the splits in *Achates* hull, and the flotilla had to shelter in Skàlafjord, a port in the Faroe Islands. She underwent further repairs there.

HMS *Achates* being towed backwards for temporary repairs in Skàlafjord,
Faroe Islands by HMRT *Assurance.*

After strengthening the bulkheads, *Achates* set sail on 21 August 1941. The
journey took four days. Under cover of darkness, like a wounded beast seeking its
den, the old warrior arrived at the best repair yard in Britain – Swan Hunter on
the Tyne. It would take nine months before she would be ready to go to sea again.

CHAPTER 2

HMS *ACHATES* REFITTED

Early April, 1942

When war started in 1939, thousands of young people volunteered for the armed services. Those who wished to join the navy went to basic training establishments for six weeks in the south of England. This prepared them for serving aboard Royal Navy warships. Henry Pallet recalled his land-based naval training at HMS *Raleigh* near Devonport.[6]

I received my final instructions and railway warrant to report myself to HMS Raleigh, Torpoint, Cornwall on the 19th December 1940. At HMS Raleigh I was first "fitted up", 2 blues, 2 whites, 2 shirts, 2 collars, 1 silk, 2 caps, 2 tallies, 2 pair boots, 2 each of socks, pants, singlets, blankets, 1 hammock, 1 greatcoat, 1 oilskin, 1 knife, 1 lanyard, 1 kitbag, 1 hat box, 1 housewife (the wallet containing needles, thread, buttons, pins etc.), and was told: 'This is your gear. In future you buy your own, for which you will receive three pence a day on your pay.

The three months at Raleigh I accepted and enjoyed and did well. The training consisted of drill with arms, gunnery, naval procedure, naval jargon, navigation, Morse, semaphore, sailing, knots and splicing, ship and watch procedure. It was usual procedure that all men were assigned to one of the Naval Divisions: Chatham, Portsmouth, or Devonport...

At the beginning of April 1942, HMS *Achates* – so damaged nine months previously – was now a new vessel with new technologies. And, interestingly, it was through the generosity of the people of Halesowen in the West Midlands that the destroyer's repair bill was funded. They had collected £330,000 through a government led scheme–*Warship Week*.

Towns, small and large, were encouraged to raise money to contribute to the war effort. Halesowen chose to sponsor HMS *Achates*.

All that *Achates* required now was a crew. A large proportion of them came from HMS *Pembroke*, the training base in Chatham. In addition to these newly-trained young lads were experienced officers and seamen. Her crew complement of 193 came from every corner of Britain.

The *Achates* captain was Lieutenant Commander AA Tait.[7] He hailed from Birkenhead. On the day of commissioning, he greeted the new crew who were stood to attention in ranks on the pier. He told them what he expected of them, which was the best effort they could provide. The crew went on board and the captain read out *The Articles of War*.[8] This was a list of regulations describing how a military force ought to behave itself in times of war.

After a service of dedication and blessing, the crew took stores on board. They were to start a fortnight of sea trials.

Friday, 24 April, 1942

On 24 April HMS *Achates* left Tyneside for Loch Ewe, where she would be located until the beginning of May. The crew were still familiarising themselves with the boat and practising procedures for 'action stations'. They had a new weapon on board, the 'Hedgehog'. This was an anti-submarine device which projected up to 24 spigot mortars to a distance of 250 yards ahead of the ship when attacking a U-boat. HJ Scott-Douglas, who was aboard HMS *Achates*, remembered these days:[9]

We left the Tyne and went round to Loch Ewe for working up, exercises, and practice with our new weapon, a hedgehog that threw 24 bombs ahead of the ship to sink submarines. After some submarine sweeps in the Minches we returned to Gourock on the Clyde which was the base for the Clyde Special Escort Group. We now prepared for our first convoy to Russia. It was P.Q.16 in May 1942. My 19th birthday had just passed. We escorted the convoy to Iceland where it would join up with the American section; we stayed at Seydis Fiord until the convoy was assembled…at this time of the year it was 24hrs. daylight—no darkness. The sun sank to the horizon, travelled to the east, and rose again. It was never out of sight.

HMS *Achates* was well-armed with two 4.7" guns, two two-pound pom-poms, four torpedo tubes, four depth-charge throwers, and two depth-charge traps at the stern. She also had radar technology installed—the common Type 291, and the more recent and more advanced Type 271. Type 271 could identify a surfaced U-boat three miles distant, and a protruding periscope 900 yards away.

A 'Hedgehog', a 24 barrelled anti-submarine mortar

A full twenty-four pattern just fired from a naval ship. Seven of the bombs have already hit the water, and seventeen more are in mid-air.

HMS *Achates* after her refit

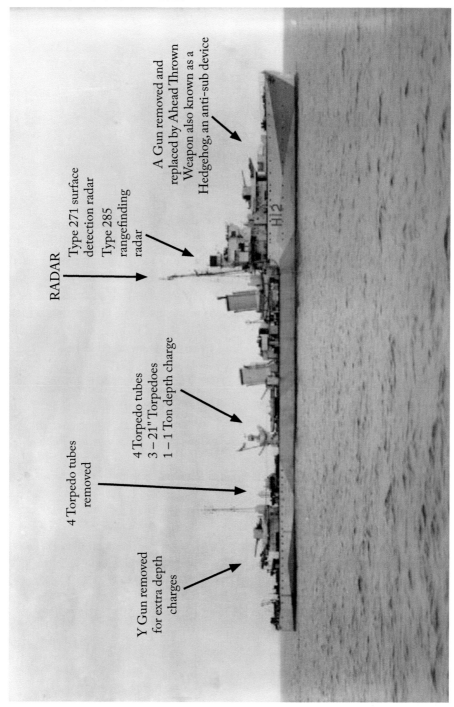

RADAR

Type 271 surface detection radar

Type 285 rangefinding radar

4 Torpedo tubes removed

4 Torpedo tubes
3 – 21" Torpedoes
1 – 1 Ton depth charge

Y Gun removed for extra depth charges

A Gun removed and replaced by Ahead Thrown Weapon also known as a Hedgehog, an anti-sub device

CHAPTER 3

CONVOY PQ16

PQ16 was the largest convoy to date to leave the shores of Britain for Russia. (PQ was the code name given to the convoys sailing from the United Kingdom to North Russia, designated so because Commander PQ Richards was tasked with writing instructions for organising and routing convoys. QP was the code given to the convoy's return journey.) Thirty merchant ships, plus a CAM (Catapult Aircraft Merchant Ship), were to rendezvous with five others which were already in Iceland. This is what Herbert Geoffrey Hall, who sailed from the Clyde in early May on the merchant ship *Ocean Voice*, recorded in his diary:[10]

> *From the Clyde we went up the coast to Loch Ewe whence I was able to get fresh views of many of my old friends, the hills of Scotland, and especially the Cuillin of Skye.*
>
> *The convoy was made up in Loch Ewe and we were made Commodore Ship, i.e., we carried the Commodore and his staff of Naval ratings, and we led the convoy. So, to Iceland where again I enjoyed the rugged mountainous scenery and we stayed for about a week, all the time on 4 hours' notice, which meant staying on watches. As we could not get ashore, we were glad to set off again on the 20th May.*
>
> *Now we had a convoy of 36 Merchant ships, accompanied by many warships from cruisers to trawlers including a CAM ship, one where a merchant ship had a long ramp fitted on the foredeck from which a Hurricane fighter could be launched to do battle with enemy bombers. The main snag was that the plane could not get back, had to be ditched and hopefully the pilot be picked up. They were brave men who flew those missions.*

HMS *Empire Lawrence*, a CAM, with a fighter plane on the catapult. She was bombed and sunk by the Luftwaffe whilst sailing in Convoy PQ16 on 27 May 1942.

Thursday, 21 May, 1942

PQ16 set sail from Hvalfjord, Iceland on 21 May – 36 merchant vessels from five nations (America (21), Russia (4), Britain (9), Holland (1), and Panama (1)) were sailing to Russia with war supplies.

Before any vessel weighed anchor in Hvalfjord, a meeting was held on the quay in the Naval Control of Shipping Office. There, the 36 merchant captains met with the escort commanders. They received their sailing orders from the convoy escort commander, Richard Onslow in HMS *Ashanti, the* flagship of the Escort Force. Convoy escort commanders were always Royal Navy personnel and in overall command of the warships protecting the convoy and of the merchant navy vessels. Escort commanders were ultimately responsible for the safety of the convoy. Onslow explained to his audience the stratagem that was to be employed should they come under attack. After him, the commodore of the merchant ships spoke. It was his duty, in liaison with the Royal Navy, to ensure 'the safe and timely arrival of the convoy'. The commodore emphasised to the merchant vessel captains: the importance of keeping formation at sea; the route they would follow; avoidance tactics; and the necessity of keeping funnels from emitting smoke (at sea, it was easier for the enemy to spot smoke from a funnel than the outline of a boat); and, finally, he underlined the need to keep an effective watch.

Neither the *Achates* nor the other destroyers were in Hvalfjord on 21 May. They had departed early to fuel up in Seidisfjord, a fjord on the west coast of Iceland. It was late on 24 May when the *Achates* and the other destroyers met up with the convoy. They had been delayed by sea fog. Nevertheless, when the fog lifted it was a pleasant sight to see nine columns of merchant shipping stretching across nine miles of ocean. The Commodore was at the head of the middle column of the convoy in *Ocean Voice*, and at the head of the other columns was a British vessel.

Merchant ships in PQ16

Name	Flag	Tonnage	Notes on merchant ships
Alamar (1916)	USA	5,689	Sunk by aircraft
Alcoa Banner (1919)	USA	5,035	
American Press (1920)	USA	5,131	
American Robin (1919)	USA	5,172	
Arcos (1918)	Soviet Union	2,343	
Atlantic (1939)	UK	5,414	
RFA *Black Ranger* (A163)	UK	3,417	
Carlton (1920)	USA	5,127	Damaged by near-misses. Towed back to Iceland by Northern Spray.
Chernyshevski (1919)	Soviet Union	3,588	
City Of Joliet (1920)	USA	6,167	Sunk by aircraft
City Of Omaha (1920)	USA	6,124	
Empire Baffin (1941)	UK	6,978	Damaged by near-misses.
Empire Elgar (1942)	UK	2,847	
Empire Lawrence (1941)	UK	7,457	Sunk by aircraft. Carried a catapult and one Hawker Sea Hurricane
Empire Purcell (1942)	UK	7,049	Sunk by aircraft
Empire Selwyn (1941)	UK	7,167	
Exterminator (1924)	Panama	6,115	
Heffron (1919)	USA	7,611	
Hybert (1920)	USA	6,120	
John Randolph (1941)	USA	7,191	
Lowther Castle (1937)	UK	5,171	Sunk by aircraft

Massmar (1920)	USA	5,828	
Mauna Kea (1919)	USA	6,064	
Michigan (1920)	Panama	6,419	
Minotaur (1918)	USA	4,554	
Mormacsul (1920)	USA	5,481	Sunk by aircraft
Nemaha (1920)	USA	6,501	
Ocean Voice (1941)	UK	7,174	Convoy Commodore. Damaged by bombs but reached port
Pieter De Hoogh (1941)	Netherlands	7,168	
Revolutsioner (1936)	Soviet Union	2,900	
Richard Henry Lee (1941)	USA	7,191	
Shchors (1921)	Soviet Union	3,770	
Starii Bolshevik (1933)	Soviet Union	3,974	Damaged by bombs but reached port
Syros (1920)	USA	6,191	Sunk by U-703
West Nilus (1920)	USA	5,495	

Royal Navy Close Convoy Escort for PQ16

Name	Flag	Ship Type	Notes on RN ships
HMS *Alynbank*	Royal Navy	Anti-aircraft	Escort 23-30 May; AA ship
HMS *Hazard*	Royal Navy	Minesweeper	21-30 May; Ocean Escort
HMS *Lady Madeleine* (FY 283)	Royal Navy	ASW * Trawler	21 May; Western Local Escort
HMS *St Elstan* (FY 240)	Royal Navy	ASW * Trawler	21 May; Western Local Escort
HMS *Retriever* (FY 261)	Royal Navy	ASW * Trawler	21-25 May; Western Local Escort
HMS *Northern Spray* (FY 129)	Royal Navy	ASW * Trawler	21-26 May; Western Local Escort
HMS *Achates*	Royal Navy	Destroyer	23-30 May; Ocean Escort

* ASW - Anti-Submarine Warfare

HMS *Ashanti*	Royal Navy	Destroyer	23-30 May; Ocean Escort, Senior Officer Escort
HMS *Martin*	Royal Navy	Destroyer	23-30 May; Ocean Escort
HMS *Volunteer*	Royal Navy	Destroyer	23-30 May; Ocean Escort
ORP *Garland*	Royal Navy	Destroyer	23-30 May; Ocean Escort
HMS *Honeysuckle*	Royal Navy	Corvette	23-30 May; Ocean Escort
HMS *Roselys*	Royal Navy	Corvette	23-30 May; Ocean Escort
HMS *Starwort*	Royal Navy	Corvette	23-30 May; Ocean Escort
HMS *Hyderabad*	Royal Navy	Corvette	23-30 May; Ocean Escort
HMS *Seawolf*	Royal Navy	Submarine	23-29 May; Ocean Escort
HMS *Trident*	Royal Navy	Submarine	23-29 May; Ocean Escort
HMS *Bramble*	Royal Navy	Minesweeper	28-30 May; Eastern Local Escort
HMS *Gossamer*	Royal Navy	Minesweeper	28-30 May; Eastern Local Escort
HMS *Leda* (J93)	Royal Navy	Minesweeper	29-30 May; Eastern Local Escort
HMS *Seagull*	Royal Navy	Minesweeper	28-30 May; Eastern Local Escort
Grozni	Russian Navy	Destroyer	28-30 May; Eastern Local Escort
Kuibyshev	Russian Navy	Destroyer	28-30 May; Eastern Local Escort
Sokrushitelny	Russian Navy	Destroyer	28-30 May; Eastern Local Escort
RFA *Black Ranger* (A163)	UK	Fleet Oiler	Force "Q"
HMS *Ledbury*	Royal Navy	Destroyer	23–30 May; Force "Q" escorted RFA *Black Ranger*

PQ16 Cruiser Cover Force

Name	Flag	Ship Type	Notes
HMS *Kent*	Royal Navy	Heavy Cruiser	23 - 26 May
HMS *Norfolk*	Royal Navy	Heavy Cruiser	23 - 26 May
HMS *Liverpool*	Royal Navy	Light Cruiser	23 - 26 May
HMS *Nigeria*	Royal Navy	Light Cruiser	23 - 26 May
HMS *Marne*	Royal Navy	Destroyer	23 - 26 May
HMS *Onslow*	Royal Navy	Destroyer	23 - 26 May
HMS *Oribi*	Royal Navy	Destroyer	23 - 26 May

PQ16 Distant Covering Force (Home Fleet)

Name	Flag	Ship Type	Notes
HMS *Victorious*	Royal Navy	Aircraft Carrier	23-29 May
HMS *Duke of York*	Royal Navy	Battleship	23-29 May
USS *Washington*	USA	Battleship	23-29 May
USS *Wichita*	USA	Heavy Cruiser	23-29 May
HMS *London*	Royal Navy	Heavy Cruiser	23-29 May
HMS *Blankney*	Royal Navy	Escort Destroyer	23-29 May
HMS *Eclipse*	Royal Navy	Destroyer	23-29 May
HMS *Faulknor*	Royal Navy	Destroyer	23-29 May
HMS *Fury*	Royal Navy	Destroyer	23-29 May
HMS *Icarus*	Royal Navy	Destroyer	23-29 May
HMS *Intrepid*	Royal Navy	Destroyer	23-29 May
HMS *Lamerton*	Royal Navy	Escort Destroyer	23-29 May
HMS *Middleton*	Royal Navy	Escort Destroyer	23-29 May
HMS *Wheatland*	Royal Navy	Escort Destroyer	23-29 May

USS *Mayrant*	USA	Destroyer	24-29 May
USS *Rhind*	USA	Destroyer	24-29 May
USS *Rowan*	USA	Destroyer	24-29 May
USS *Wainwright*	USA	Destroyer	24-29 May

Monday, 25 May, 1942

On 25 May, four days after leaving Iceland, PQ16 rendezvoused with a squadron of 4 cruisers and 3 destroyers under the command of Rear Admiral Harold Burrough who was in the cruiser HMS *Nigeria*. HMS *Nigeria* was familiar with the waters around the Norwegian coast and had a celebrated history there. A year previously, in August 1941, she was part of the navy group which captured the German weather ship, the *Laurenberg*, north-east of Jan Myan Island.

They seized code books and parts of an Enigma machine. This took place a few weeks after HMS *Bulldog* had seized a complete Enigma device from U-110 south of Iceland. The machine and the code books provided Alan Turing and his group in Bletchley Park with vital information. They were able to break the German code and read U-boat messages for several weeks.

The 4 cruisers and the 3 destroyers under Burrough's command took their positions amongst PQ 16's columns to provide support and protection against attack from U-boats, the Luftwaffe, and warships. The admiralty in London believed the greatest danger would come from the German surface vessels: Admiral *Scheer* based at *Narvik*, the warship *Lützow*, the destroyer *Hans Lody*, and torpedo-boat *T7*.

On the 25th, a Focke-Wolf Condor appeared. It circled the convoy but far enough away to be out of range of British guns. Spotter planes would circle the convoy day and night as it made its way to Russia. They fed information about course and speed to the U-boats who were waiting for an opportunity to sink a merchant ship. Sometimes a Condor would land on the water for an hour or two to save fuel, and then fly off.

On the evening of 25 May, the convoy caught their first sighting of a surfaced U-boat. It dived speedily, but no order came for the destroyers to pursue it. They had to remain with the convoy. It was around 11:00pm that same evening, with the sun still shining brightly, that the first air attack came. Bombers and torpedo planes appeared like hooded crows coming to take the eyes out of the lambs. The sky became pock-marked with the fire-power of the cruisers.

Two German planes fell out of the air.

A Hurricane which had been launched from the *Empire Lawrence*, a CAM, struck down one torpedo bomber. When the attack had finished, only one convoy vessel, *The Carlton*, had been put out of action. Unfortunately, the Hurricane had also been hit, with the pilot having to bale out. The Russian-born British war correspondent, Alexander Werth, was on board HMS *Honeysuckle*, commanded by Captain Roy Dykes. This is what Werth wrote about the incident:[11]

> *They appeared in the distance, on the starboard side, low above the water: three – four – five, then three more, then four or five after that, further to the right. We were all on deck – the R.A.F. boys, with their tin hats, and the deck-hands, the cabin boys – and we counted and watched. Eleven, twelve, thirteen…*
>
> *Something was already happening ahead of us. The gunners had rushed up to the gun-turrets. The two cruisers which had suddenly joined us earlier in the day and the destroyers on the edge of the convoy were firing like mad. It was a beautiful bright day, the sea calm and blue like the Mediterranean, and the sky was now dotted with specks of smoke from the flak shells.*
>
> *They went in a half-circle round the front of the convoy then, after a few seconds of suspense, they came right out of the sun. They swooped over us, two or three in succession, and from their yellow bellies the yellow eggs dropped, slowly, obscenely. They were after the cruisers, in the middle of the convoy.*
>
> *The tracer-bullets from our Oerlikons were rushing at the yellow belly of the Junker 88 as he swooped over us. A loud squeal, growing louder and louder, and then the explosion, as a stick of bombs landed between us and the destroyer, on the port side. Three pillars of water went high up in the air, and the ship shook. As he dived, almost to the water level, our tracer-bullets followed him, but he got out of their way and on the bridge Captain Dykes, wearing a wide navy-blue beret, was waving and shouting frantically: 'Don't fire so low! You're hitting the next ship'…*

Werth also revealed that it was not the Germans who had downed the Hurricane:

> *Meantime the catapult Hurricane on the Empire Lawrence had leaped swiftly into the air, in pursuit of the dive-bombers. Swiftly it went in a wide circle round the convoy ready to pounce on one of them; but here something unfortunate happened; one of the American cargoes, no doubt mistaking the Hurricane for a German plane, fired what gun or machine gun it had at him, and the next thing we saw was the pilot baling out by parachute, with nothing to show for his exploit, and with the Hurricane nothing to show for its £5,000.*

The ice and the intense cold were constantly on the mind of each sailor on the Russian Convoys because they knew that if they fell into the water they would freeze to death in a matter of minutes, as Captain Dykes of HMS *Honeysuckle* explained:[12]

If you take a frozen package from your deep freezer and hold it in your hand, in a matter of seconds your fingers will start to hurt, and the tips will start to turn blue. It is very painful and if you don't drop it quickly, it will stick to your hand. Think of the short seconds taken for that situation to happen, and then relate it to a man thrown from his ship as it blows up, into a sea that has ice sludge floating on the surface...It was so cold, you lost your breath and couldn't call out. You could not survive.

An ice field in the Arctic

Captain Dykes continued:

The decks would be very slippery with ice, and the ship would be rolling, but you daren't touch the rails because if you did, you would lose your skin. The hardest part was trying to get some rest. We had 24 hours of daylight and we were constantly attacked, not by single aircraft but hundreds at a time.

After the attack, the convoy encountered an ice field. For the sailors, the shriek of the ice as it scoured the sides of the boat was much preferable to the screech of Nazi engines attacking from the air.

CHAPTER 4

U-BOATS

Tuesday, 26 May, 1942

Around 03:00 on the morning of Tuesday 26 May, sonar echoes were picked up from a U-boat which had penetrated Convoy PQ16. Kapitän-leutenant Heinz Bielfeld in *U-703* torpedoed the *Syros*, an American merchant ship. The *Syros* was the last ship in the seventh column. She sank rapidly. Here is a description of the event:[13]

> *At 02:59 hours on 26 May 1942 the Syros (Master, Cornelius Albert Holmes) in convoy PQ-16 was hit on the port side by two torpedoes from U-703 about 200 miles southwest of Bear Island. The first torpedo had been spotted by other ships in convoy and was fired on, but it struck abreast of her stack in the engine room and was followed by a second torpedo which hit at the number 2 hatch, causing the ammunition in the cargo to explode. The ship broke in two and sank within 80 seconds. The eight officers, 30 crewmen and two armed guards were not able to abandon ship in the lifeboats because both on the port side had been destroyed by the explosions, and the others could not be launched in time. The survivors left on three rafts or jumped overboard and clung to wreckage until they were picked up by HMS Hazard (Lt Cdr J.R.A. Seymour, RN) and landed at Murmansk, but two of them died of exposure and were buried at sea. The master, two officers, eight crewmen and an armed guard were lost.*

The *Achates* went in pursuit of *U-703*. However, Kapitänleutnant Heinz Bielfield knew that the ASDIC (Anti-Submarine Detection Investigation Committee – an underwater ear) did not work well where there were strata of water at different temperature levels (*thermoclines*). He submerged his craft to a depth which was colder than the sea temperature around the *Achates*.

The destroyer did not locate *U-703*.

Whilst the *Achates* was hunting U-703, Admiral Burrough[14] who was in the light cruiser HMS Nigeria, turned away from the middle of the convoy and sailed speedily to the north at 20 knots (23 mph), a move which mystified both the Americans and the Russians. It was later alleged that the move was to assist Convoy QP12 which was on its return journey from Russia. However, Convoy PQ16's defensive firepower had been diminished by Admiral Burrough's action. (Perhaps the truth of the matter was that it was dangerous for Burrough and his escort to be left in the middle of a slow-moving convoy, the Admiralty in London being on edge having seen HMS *Trinidad* and HMS *Edinburgh* sunk earlier in the month.)

There were other U-boats circling Convoy PQ16. Two of them, *U-436* and *U-591*, fired torpedoes which passed close to a merchant ship and to HMS *Ashanti*. In spite of this, no damage was inflicted. In his book, *Sonar: Detector of Submerged Submarines*, AP Hilar relates:[15]

(1) Sound travelling in warm surface water bends sharply downward when it passes through a thermocline (a region where temperature decreases sharply with depth) and results in very weak echoes being returned from submarines beneath the thermocline,
(2) …thermoclines may cause loss of Sonar contact,
(3) …U-boats may hide under thermoclines.

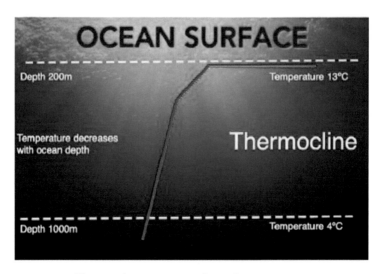

Thermoclines may cause loss of sonar contact

U-boats could safely descend to depths of 90-100 metres. Some commanders would descend to 200 metres in extremis, and according to reports survived the experience.

However, the 'collapse depth' (the depth at which a U-boat would split apart at the seams because of water pressure) was calculated to be between 200-280 meters (660-20 feet). *The Submarine Commander's Handbook* provided U-boat captains with detailed information on self-preservation as seen in the extract below: [16]

Submarine Commander's Handbook

Geheim!
Entered in the "TOK" List of Secret Records ("TOK" = "Torpedo [-boat] Command") under current number 5; Submarine "U2326."

THE SUBMARINE COMMANDER'S HANDBOOK
("U.Kdt.Hdb.")
Incorporated in the Secret Archives
under Heading IV, No. 4
Command 32, Submarine Flotilla

1942
New Edition 1943
(comprising Amendments Nos. 1-11)
High Command of the Navy

D.V. No. 906

Section IV

Action to be taken in case of Defensive Action and Pursuit by the Enemy.

246.) The object of the enemy anti-submarine defence and offensive action is the destruction of the submarine, either by direct armed attack underwater, or by keeping the submarine underwater to the point of exhaustion, and then destroying it when it surfaces.

247.) As a matter of principle, the submarine which is the object of enemy underwater pursuit should behave in such a way that it remains active, and should try to make good its escape by availing itself of every possibility, instead of simply waiting, and lying passively at the bottom. Activity on the part of the submarine always offers the best chances of shaking off the enemy.

248.) In all operations, the chief danger for the submarine is at the beginning, when the enemy, having witnessed the attack by the submarine, and seen it submerge, is best able to assess its position, and the submarine has not yet reached any great depth.

Consequently, if the submarine has been detected, it should leave the scene of the attack, or the spot where it has submerged, at full speed, and go deep down without troubling about the possibility of being sound-located.

249.) Free

A. What to do when pursued by Sound Location.

250.) Attention is called to the general remarks concerning enemy sound location: Section I, B, II, Nos. 46 to 54.

Suggestions as to the possibilities of shaking off the enemy:

a) Take the D/F sound location of the enemy astern.

b) Eliminate all sources of noise in the submarine: stop all auxiliary machinery which is not indispensable (pumps, ventilators, compressors, periscope motor, gyroscopic compass – above all, the secondary gyroscopes – etc.); main rudder and hydroplane should be operated by hand; pumping out, and trimming, with air; depth steering as far as possible only by head list, and then trimming by hand.

c) Absolute silence of the crew on board the submarine; speaking in low tones, working silently, moving about in stockinged feet, etc.

d) Go down very deep; the deeper the position of the submarine, the greater the probability of being incorrectly sound-located.

e) Run out and double at a good distance, and then make off on a straight course, in order to get well away from the pursuing enemy forces. Do not double frequently, or continually zigzag, because this results in loss of distance.

f) If possible, get away in the wake of the enemy's screw, on account of the effective interference level affecting his reception in sound location.

g) Accelerate your speed when the enemy accelerates (or when depth charges are detonated), and stop, or slow down to minimum r.p.m. of the engine, when the enemy stops.

Life on board a U-boat

It was not pleasant on board a U-boat. The crew lived inside a cylinder. Under the deck were diving tanks, a battery room, a torpedo room, a diesel engine, and electric motors. There was not much '*lebensraum*'.

Apart from existing inside a claustrophobic cylinder, the crew would suffer from poor air quality. There was no mechanism underwater to remove carbon dioxide from the submarine, nor one for increasing the amount of oxygen. These developments came later in the war. However, each sailor in a U-boat had their own personal apparatus which they could put on to remove carbon dioxide from the air, until they could surface.

Strangely, there was no place on board to store vegetables and they would rot quickly. Neither did they receive training on how to preserve or store vegetables. On one occasion, a U-boat was captured and beached in Iceland. The two British officers who went on board to inspect it had to wear breathing apparatus because of the stench inside.

When they entered, they waded in water up to their knees. In the foul liquid were the remains of vomit from seasick German sailors. In addition, there was human excrement, German black bread, and sailing through this disagreeable broth was spilt gruel. The malodour was dreadful according to the officers.[17] Perhaps, the state of the U-boat is not so surprising when we realise that there was only one WC on board for a crew of 50. The crew frequently resorted to using pails.

According to Royal Navy experts, the submarines themselves were well-built. However, the on-board systems were basic. Some believed the reason for this was the German view that in time of war it was easier to train replacement sailors on a U-boat if the systems were straightforward, especially if the personnel were not well-educated.

Despite the gravity of war, there were humorous incidents. Jak Showell remembers his father, a U-boat captain, telling him about an incident in Spitzbergen. The crew went ashore and discovered an abandoned hotel with an intact stock of spirits. When the U-boat commander heard about this, he warned the crew that not one bottle of alcohol was to be brought aboard the ship. The crew, however, knew that there was an 88mm gun on deck, and that the barrel was just wide enough to allow several bottles of whisky to be stored within.[18]

U-boat success in targeting ships did not last the length of the war though. In 1940, each U-boat at sea was sinking on average up to 6 merchant ships each month. In 1942, on average, U-boat success rates were reduced to one merchant ship per month. Many attribute this statistic to two innovations – Radar and Huff-Duff. With radar, Royal Navy ships and RAF planes could identify U-boats on their screens during the darkness of the night. The Huff-Duff (High Frequency Direction Finder) could detect the location of a radio transmission. U-boats had to send a short radio message to their shore base each time they were going to launch an attack on a vessel. That short radio transmission was sufficient for Huff-Duff to locate the submarine.

CHAPTER 5

AIR ATTACKS ON PQ16

Tuesday, 26 May 1942

On the morning of 26 May, the weather was muggy. Despite the low cloud base, the Luftwaffe began their attacks. They continued from early morning until 18:00. In the final attack, seven torpedo bombers appeared. However, PQ16 put up a fierce defensive wall and routed them.

Around midday, HMS *Achates'* ASDIC picked up a *U-boat* to starboard and increased speed to close in on the submarine. Every binocular was scanning the ocean, and one observer spotted a black speck on the horizon. After an interval, the black speck transformed into the shape of a conning tower. *Achates* was now three miles from the target. The *U-boat* spotted her and submerged. Although *Achates* performed a square search according to the drill, she could not locate the *U-boat*. But just as she was about to cease searching, the ASDIC operator picked up the sound of torpedoes tearing towards the destroyer. Two torpedo wakes were spotted. The captain altered course swiftly and the torpedoes travelled past the ship. A square search was carried out once more. No contacts were made with the *U-boat* and the *Achates* returned to the defensive screen.

Wednesday, 27 May 1942

On this day, because of the ice, the convoy had to sail much closer to Norway's North Cape. North Cape is the most northerly point on the continent of Europe and for the convoys the place closest to Banak, a Luftwaffe base.

In the early hours of 27 May, the weather was good. The first attack came at 03:20. Surprisingly, the Germans did no damage in this initial air assault. However, after this and for ten hours continuously between 11:15 and 21:00, wave after wave of dive bombers and torpedo bombers arrived. These two groups worked together. The torpedo bombers would circle the convoy. The dive bombers would rise high above the convoy, hiding themselves in

Location of Banak Airport in Northern Norway

the clouds. Their focus would be on one particular vessel and, attacking jointly, they conspired to send the cargo ship to the bottom of the ocean.

A Heinkel HE 111 on a snow-covered airfield in Russia

Although the Royal Navy could see where the German planes were on their radar screens, they were out of range until the two fighter groups approached in a joint attack. This occasioned a fearful hail of tracers and shells from the destroyers which were steaming up and down the convoy launching cascades of metal to form a defensive wall against the enemy. The sounds of war boomed – up and down, port and starboard. A radio officer on SS Atlantic described the sound of a cruiser's gun being fired:

One of the cruisers fired its 15mm (six-inch) guns straight over us, and the ear-shattering 'crack' had to be experienced to be believed. It shook a lot of rust out of hidden spaces.

Sadly, there were boats lost – the SS *Lowther Castle* being one. Roy Dykes who was on board HMS *Honeysuckle* recorded:[19]

The Lowther Castle was hit in the bow by an aerial torpedo and it slowed it down slightly. Then it became the target for dive bombers and it was hit. The crew abandoned ship and we rescued them. We had to put what was called a sea boat down – that's a small dinghy – to pick them up, even though they had their own life boats. But one that was missing in the crew was the captain. And so, with our own dinghy in the water, we went to try and find him round the starboard side of the ship.

We found him clinging to the falls of the ship – the ropes which come from the davits and lowers the lifeboat into the sea – he was clinging to these falls (with his arms wrapped around them) and he was so frightened that he wouldn't listen to us. We tried to get him to swim a matter of a few yards to our dinghy but he wouldn't do it. He must have been so traumatised as a result of that morning's attacks, and witnessing the destruction of the Empire Lawrence without trace on his port side and the attack on the Empire Purcell to starboard of him. The captain took no notice of our pleas to help save him.

The ship was on fire and gradually heeling over. We were bombed. We were machine-gunned. The lifeboats were machine-gunned. But in the end, we were recalled to my ship which was HMS Honeysuckle because it was getting dangerous, very dangerous. And we were about ten miles astern of the convoy, so we were isolated completely – on our own. So we had to leave him. We had no choice because of the danger to Honeysuckle. As we left, the Lowther Castle turned turtle, rolled over, and sank with the captain still holding on to the falls.

Out of a crew of 65, all were rescued except the captain. The *Alamar*, the *Mormacsul*, the *Empire Baffin*, the *Empire City of Joliet* and the *Lowther Castle* were sunk along with their valuable cargo. Other merchant ships had been set ablaze. The crews succeeded in smothering the flames, with help at times from a protection vessel. Despite the damage done, these vessels returned to their column and place in the convoy and continued their journey.

The *Garland*, a Polish destroyer, was the only ship in the Royal Navy to be badly damaged that day. A bomb exploded close to her, which in turn set off still-falling bombs, riddling her with shrapnel. Her front gun was put out of action, as was one boiler.

The *Achates* went to her aid, and a doctor and medical supplies were put on board. As the *Achates* approached the *Garland*, the sight which the crew saw shocked them. Twenty-five sailors who had been killed were laid out on the deck, as well as the 50 or so who had been wounded. The crew of the *Garland* were working like lightning trying to repair the damage. When the *Achates* came close, a young sailor was viewed hosing the deck, and the crew of the *Achates* saw the side of the *Garland* change colour from grey to red as the blood was rinsed away. They also saw this sailor pick up something from the deck. It was what remained of someone's arm.

The bomber attacks continued all afternoon. The *Ocean Voice*, the commodore's ship, was hit and set ablaze, but remained at the head of the convoy. The crew managed to bring the fire under control, which boosted the morale of the whole convoy.

The Russian vessel, *Starii Bolshevik*, also displayed her nerve. About midday, after a bomber attack, a fire threatened to ignite her cargo of munitions. The Russian crew, male and female, worked tenaciously to smother the fire.

The *Empire Purcell*, on her maiden voyage, also had a cargo of munitions, but she was not so fortunate as the *Starii Bolshevik*. Two bombs entered *No. 2 hold*, exploded, and started an inferno. At the same time, two bombs struck her superstructure. Hatches and beams flew into the air. The bunker bulkhead was damaged and an avalanche of coal poured into the area where the stokers were working. Water cascaded into the engine room from damaged pipes and valves. The engineers stopped the vessel. Captain Stephenson knew that the cargo of munitions could explode at any moment and gave the order to abandon ship.

The *Empire Purcell* on fire following the Luftwaffe attacks.

Unfortunately, one of the lifeboats fell into the sea. Frozen davit ropes had become brittle and snapped. The sailors trapped underneath the lifeboat were all saved. However, six others who had fallen into the icy waters did not survive. Two others were lost in the confusion.

There was one other lifeboat available. Captain Stephenson and some officers managed to lower this one. They and several of the crew managed to escape before the *Empire Purcell* blew up 'with a stunning explosion'.

Before the end of the 27th, two Heinkels appeared and fired a torpedo each. The convoy took evasive action with the intention of letting the torpedoes run harmlessly by. However, one ship was struck – the *Ocean Voice*, the commodore's vessel. She did not go down, but the damage was so serious that Commodore Gale had to hand convoy control to Vice Commodore JT Hair on the *Empire Selwyn*. The bridge on the *Ocean Voice* had been obliterated. Despite the worst prognosis she survived and reached port with the convoy.

No Royal Navy vessel was lost, but the crew of the *Achates* and those of the other protection vessels were exhausted. They had three more days of sailing before they would reach Murmansk, and they knew that they would have to use their bullets and shells sparingly. This was confirmed when the Escort Commander signalled that each ship had to conserve its munitions. One report details the events of this day from dawn to dusk:[20]

After an air attack which did no harm at 03:20, 27th May, course had to be altered to the south-eastward for a couple of hours to avoid heavy pack ice. At 11:15 there started a series of attacks by a large number of Ju.88s which continued with little respite till 21:30; six merchant ships were lost, and three, in addition to the Garland, suffered damage. The Alynbank recorded attacks by 108 aircraft on this day, and 120 sticks of bombs or torpedoes were heard to explode.

The dive bombing attacks were pressed well home from broken cloud at 3,000 feet and the enemy was assisted by an intermittent filmy haze at about 1,500 feet, which made them very difficult to see.

The first casualty occurred at 13:10, when S.S. Alamar was hit by two bombs and set on fire; five minutes later the Mormacsul was damaged by two near misses. Both ships sank at 13:30, survivors being rescued by escort craft. Between 14:05 and 14:10, five direct hits sank the Empire Lawrence, and another started a fire in the Starii Bolshevik, which was successfully fought by her crew for 36 hours: near misses damaged the Empire Baffin, O.R.P. Garland, and the City of Joliet, the last so badly that she had to be abandoned next morning. Great courage and determination were shown by the smaller escort vessels in rescuing survivors from the ships which had been sunk, though subjected to deliberate heavy dive-bombing while doing so.

Soon after these attacks, ice conditions allowed a more northerly course and at 14:35 Commander Onslow ordered the convoy to steer 060°; there appeared to be more cloud in that direction, and he also hoped that the increased distance from the enemy's airfields would diminish the weight of the air attacks next day.

During the rest of the afternoon there was a lull in the action – except for one ineffective attack by eight Ju.88s – till 19:45, when heavy divebombing recommenced, accompanied by attacks by torpedo aircraft. The Empire Purcell was hit by bombs and later blew up, the Lowther Castle was torpedoed and sunk, and the Commodore's ship, the Ocean Voice, received a direct hit which set her on fire and tore away 20 feet of her side plating abreast No. 1 hold within two feet of the water line. Fortunately the sea remained calm.

'I had little hopes of her survival,' wrote Commander Onslow subsequently, 'but this gallant ship maintained her station, fought her fire, and with God's help arrived at her destination.'

There were no further attacks after 21:30 that day; but two Blohm and Voss float planes could be seen ominously circling the horizon. The situation appeared far from rosy. Five ships had been lost. The City of Joliet was settling by the bows and the Ocean Voice appeared unlikely to remain afloat much longer. The Garland was so seriously damaged that she was detached later in the evening to make her own way to Murmansk at high speed. 'With another three days to go and 20 per cent of the convoy already lost,' to quote Commander Onslow, 'I felt far from optimistic. The question of ammunition began to worry me badly. I ordered all ships to exercise strict economy and restricted controlled fire in the Ashanti to one mounting at a time. We were all inspired however by the parade ground rigidity of the convoy's station keeping, including Ocean Voice and Starii Bolshevik who were both billowing smoke from their foreholds.'

The *Achates* and the rest of the convoy were grateful for the falling fog which hid them from the enemy. However, although the fog cover was a friend, it was also a dangerous friend. With fog comes a drop in temperature, and the sailors had to be watchful that the forming ice did not damage equipment nor imbalance the ship. Despite everything the crew managed to catch some sleep. The Luftwaffe were unable to maintain their attacks. Wednesday 27 April was about to pass. It had been a day without mercy.

Thursday 28 to Friday 29 May, 1942

There was one attack on the 28th and this did not begin until 21:30. Earlier in the day, the convoy had greeted three Russian destroyers – the *Grozni*, the *Sokrushilelni*, and the *Kuibishev* – which had arrived to provide support. This added to the AA (Anti-Aircraft) firepower of the convoy. When the Luftwaffe arrived, the Russians fired upon them, sending up a colossal defensive wall. This gave the convoy an uplift, and it alarmed the Germans. The Russians had arrived at an opportune moment.

Chipping ice from ventilators and lockers

When the bombers flew back to their Norwegian base, the convoy had an opportunity to reorganise above and below deck. Above deck, shell cases were swept over the side. It was considered inappropriate, given the onslaught they had just suffered, to do the customary recycling collection. Below deck, equipment, hoses, and cables were strewn. The twists and turns vessels had made trying to avoid bomber and torpedo attacks had buckled sailors' lockers and their personal effects had been scattered across the sleeping quarters.

On deck, the ice was now forming quickly and thickly. Walking had become dangerous. This was one reason the ice had to be fragmented. Secondly, if too much ice formed upon a ship's mast and tackle, the equilibrium of the boat could be compromised, something a captain would not want to happen to his vessel. Another task which had to be carried out was to smear a specialist grease over arms and munitions to protect them from the frost.

Morale amongst the convoy crew was boosted after this clean-up. Vessels were now shipshape for a little while at least.

In the small hours of Friday 29 May, the Germans attacked. However, once again, the Luftwaffe did little damage to the convoy which was now 140 miles north-east of the Kola Inlet. On the evening of the 29th Captain Crombie, who commanded the 1st Minesweeping Flotilla based in Kola, rendezvoused with PQ16. There were five other escort ships with him, and they were to accompany six merchant vessels to Archangel. Archangel, in the White Sea, was around 400 nautical miles away and in May free of ice and open to vessels.

CHAPTER 6

DESIRED HAVEN

Saturday 30 and Sunday 31 May, 1942

During the last two days of May, as PQ16 neared Murmansk, there were further attacks by Junkers and Heinkels. They were not so venomous as previous efforts because the Germans fired their torpedoes and dropped their bombs a good distance from the merchant vessels. Not one hit their targets. However, a torpedo did pass perilously close to the stern of HMS *Achates*.

Late on Saturday evening, 30 May, the convoy divided. Six merchant ships went with Captain Crombie to Archangel, and Crombie took with him two Royal Navy vessels, the *Martin* and the *Alynbank*. This was a blow to Richard Onslow, PQ16 commander, as he was losing the only two ships which were capable of raising their guns high enough to fire at planes at high altitude. The consequence was that the remaining protection vessels had to engage the Luftwaffe at closer quarters and with lighter guns.

Cargo being unloaded at Murmansk

Lorry being unloaded at Murmansk docks

The *Achates* and the other vessels in PQ16 were now close to the Kola Inlet, a sheltered fjord around 35 miles in length. About 18 miles from Murmansk, and halfway up the inlet, is Vaenga Bay. Here, the Royal Navy protection vessels anchored and here the wounded received medical aid, albeit at a very basic level. On the west side of the inlet was Polyarnoe where the Russians were based. Facilities were much better there.

The place name Murmansk may come from the old Norse word *Murman*, reckoned to mean the North Men or Normans. Today, Murmansk is the world's largest city north of the Arctic Circle with around 270,000 inhabitants. In 1942, the city had between three to four miles of harbour area, much of which had been damaged because of the war. The city was only 113 miles (182 km) from the border with Finland and 67 miles (108 km) from Norway's border. Murmansk was so close to the German airforce that they could easily mount an attack on the port. Some described Murmansk as a camp with wooden huts scattered here and there.

However, it did have buildings constructed of brick and concrete. On Stalin Avenue, were buildings six and ten storeys high.

PQ16 arrives at Murmansk and Archangel

Twenty-seven merchant vessels out of 35 had reached Russia – 21 to Murmansk on 30 May and 6 to Archangel on 1 June. In the words of Admiral Tovey, Commander of the Home Fleet, it was 'beyond expectations'. During PQ16's voyage, one vessel was sunk by *U-703*, six by bombers, and one by a mine. The enemy had carried out 288 air attacks. Churchill had said that if half managed through safely that would be a success. And, although 43,205 tons of shipping had been sunk with cargo including 147 tanks, 77 planes, and 770 vehicles, more than three quarters of the merchant vessels reached their destination. The journey from Iceland had taken ten days.

It had been a terrible baptism for most on the *Achates*, especially between 25th and 29th May, when shoal after shoal of Luftwaffe aircraft attacked, resulting in the sinking of seven merchant vessels.

However, if the crew of the Achates anticipated a cessation of air attacks and a warm welcome from the Russians, they were mistaken. The danger of air-attack was still present as the port was perilously close to German lines. The Germans were so close they could raid anytime they wished. Indeed, on the way into the inlet, between Polyarnoe and Murmansk, the convoy saw five ships which had been destroyed by bombs and which were now half submerged. The five vessels were all British.

There was a feeling amongst the British sailors that the Russians were tholing them rather than warmly welcoming them. Here is how Alexander Rothney, a radio operator on board a merchant ship, wrote about a dance he attended in Murmansk:[21]

> *We soon sensed we were tolerated rather than welcomed and left. It may have been that the locals were chary of appearing too friendly in case they fell foul of the police. We had heard that Russians suspected of being friendly with foreigners were liable to be arrested and imprisoned.*

The welcome which British sailors received from the Russians bordered on animosity in the opinion of many. And the Russian government officials were the most guilty. Day and night armed guards encompassed the docks to ensure there was no communication between sailors and local inhabitants. When British sailors had the opportunity to go beyond the dockland area into the city itself, they had to present their paybooks to the guards. The guards aimed their guns at the sailors whilst their papers were being checked.

The Russian workers in the dock areas comprised criminals, political prisoners, and women. The women were highly skilled in riveting, ship repairs, and plating. It was difficult to immediately recognise them as female because of their dress and strength.

In the city of Murmansk itself, there was little activity. The wooden houses were gloomy and basic without any charm. It did not take long until the British sailors organised a black market with 'luxury' items for sale from the ship's NAAFI – cigarettes, soap, chocolate bars (or *nutty* as the sailors called it). These items were sold for ridiculous prices. The British 'business men' could not step far from the dock gates until they were surrounded by children who were go-betweens for that black market.

Although there was high demand for the 'luxury' items, the daily food on board the *Achates* was diminishing. This was because a large part of their stores had been given to survivors from sunken vessels. The result was the *Achates* crew was often fed black bread and yak meat.

There was one thing in particular which especially annoyed the sailors when in Murmansk. They had endangered their lives to deliver stores and goods for the Russians, but now they were seeing the Russians carelessly handling these items when hoisting them from ships' holds.

We should perhaps have a little compassion towards the Russian workers when we understand their situation. Women were to be seen everywhere and they were the dockers for the most part. They had brutal shifts of 24 hours on and then 24 hours off. Although there were males, they were not the most healthy of individuals. Fit men had long gone to fight at the front. Many of the dockers were there against their will, and starving. One story tells of a docker who was caught eating from a can of tinned meat which had fallen out of a cargo net and had split open. A guard arrested him, took him behind a mound of recently landed goods and shot him. Little wonder the sailors felt that Murmansk was a gloomy, inhospitable destination.

However, despite this side of things, the courage and effort of the Russians against the Germans was remarkable. They kept the railway line between Archangel, Murmansk, and Moscow open despite the venomous attacks of the Nazis. In some places the railway was about 50 miles away from the front which stretched across the Finnish border, and the Germans were 2:1 stronger. As soon as an air attack on the railway was past, squads of repairers would appear and the track would be soon mended, permitting the cargoes to move south.

Many of the sailors considered that Murmansk and Archangel were the worst two ports they visited. The gloom, the mistrust, the suspicion, the corruption, and the ungratefulness all combined to create this impression of the port.

Here is how Calum MacLeod from Carloway, Isle of Lewis recorded his feelings in this piece of poetry he wrote:[22]

The Scapa-Kola Inlet Run: 1942

But Russia is not the place for succour or advice,
Its disregard for pain and life is Stalin's harsh device,
In the history of warfare no country persevered,
With an ally so suspicious, tactless and austere.

Polyarno is their naval base, a safe and sheltered port,
But our exhausted escortmen are barred from this resort,
Instead disquietly we are forced to bleak cold Rosta Bay,
Or to the loathsome Vaenga where the escort oiler lay.

En route to a rowing competition, Murmansk. Taken from the deck of the *Achates*.

Rowing competition, Murmansk. Taken from the deck of the *Achates*.

There was one thing which raised the spirits of the Royal Navy crews, and this was the regatta, in which crews from different ships rowed against each other. Day and night the crews would be honing their skills and their times in the rowing boats. In one of these competitions, the *Achates* came very close to winning. Captain A.H.T. Johns himself took part as coxswain of the rowing skiff.

There were other pastimes such as football and concerts. The concerts were delivered via the ships SRE (Sound Reproduction System) and lifted crew morale. The performances via ship's radio were to all intents ceilidhs, with humorous stories, songs, poetry, and quick-witted banter. The subject-matter of the songs was usually a recent incident. All these activities helped naval personnel pass the time and maintain morale whilst merchant vessel cargo was being unloaded and before receiving orders to return to the United Kingdom.

CHAPTER 7

LEAVING MURMANSK

Saturday 27 June to Saturday 4 July, 1942

The *Achates* sailed from Murmansk on 27 June, having been moored for almost a month. It was returning as part of the defensive screen for the thirty-five merchant vessels in QP13. One section of the convoy had sailed from Archangel (400 nautical miles away) on 26 June aiming to join up with the Murmansk group on 28 June. Most of the merchant ships were returning empty, apart from the Soviet vessels which were carrying timber. The ships of QP13 were variously destined for the United Kingdom, Iceland and North America.

Convoy QP13 sailed from Murmansk in concurrence with PQ17's departure from Iceland. The Admiralty considered that both convoys would benefit from the strengthened defensive screen of PQ17, which comprised: the aircraft carrier HMS *Victorious*; the battleship HMS *Duke of York*; the cruisers *Cumberland* and *Nigeria*; the destroyers *Ashanti, Douglas, Faulknor, Mame, Onslaught, and Onslow;* the American battleship USS *Washington;* and the American destroyers *Mayrant* and *Rhind*. PQ17 was under the command of Admiral John Tovey whose flagship was the *Duke of York*.

QP13's defensive screen was less formidable. It comprised: the anti-aircraft ship *Alynbank*; the destroyers *Achates, Garland, Inglefield, Intrepid,* and *Volunteer;* the minesweepers *Hussar* and *Niger;* and the corvettes *Honeysuckle, Hyderabad, Roselys,* and *Starwort*.

The weather was overcast on their return journey to Britain; this helped to shield the convoy from enemy attack. In addition, QP13 had the opportunity to sail a more northerly course and, thus, be further away from the German airfields in the north of Norway. Icebergs had melted due to the seasonal increase in temperature. However, because they were much further north, they were on the edge of the polar icecap and there were days when icebergs and ice fields surrounded them, making progress slow.

Ships returning to Britain from Russia frequently took with them survivors of vessels which had previously gone down. Some of the crew of HMS *Edinburgh* were sailing back on the *Achates*. The *Edinburgh* had been returning home with 465 gold ingots in 93 wooden crates when three German destroyers sank her near *Bjørna* (Bear island) on 2 May, 1942. This cargo had a value of £70 million, part-payment for the war supplies convoys were transporting to Russia.

As well as carrying sailors from HMS *Edinburgh*, the *Achates* carried Russian officers, and a Russian dog which the *Achates'* crew had somehow managed to obtain whilst they were in Murmansk. Timoshenko was the name given to the dog, named after one of Russia's most famous generals. Unfortunately, in a rough sea, Timoshenko fell over the ship's side. This caused the crew no little amount of distress. The Russian officers heard that Timoshenko was dead and they also began to mourn this loss. However, they thought that it was the general who had died and began to drown their sorrows in vodka, toasting him with great affection. They took a while celebrating the loss of Timoshenko before they realised that it was the dog which had died.

The British and Russian officers on board the *Achates* engaged in banter which enhanced relationships. The Royal Naval officers adjusted their names: *Peyton Jones* was now *Peytonovich Joneski*, *Eric Marland Erico Marlandovitch*, and *James MacFarland Jameski Macfarlandochov*. The 'Russian' names of the British officers were on their letter racks in the wardroom and when the *Achates* returned to the Clyde, one of the newspaper reporters who had come on board noticed this and soon the story appeared in the daily newspapers.

HMS *Achates'* homeward journey in QP13 saw little enemy action. The Kriegsmarine (German Navy) strategy was to attack convoys which were laden with war goods for Russia and to leave unmolested unladen convoys on their homeward journey. This was what happened to QP13. *Admiral Nordmeer* (Admiral of the Northern Waters), Hubert Schmundt, ordered German forces to ignore the empty westbound ships and focus on the loaded ships of eastbound convoy PQ17.

However, QP13 was not without incident. On 2 July the 35 ships in the convoy divided off the coast of Iceland. Sixteen ships turned south for Loch Ewe. The other 19 vessels rounded the north of Iceland heading for Reykjavik and North America. However, on 5 July a horrendous incident took place involving six of the ships making for Reykjavik. Fog fell, and, in poor visibility, the minesweeper HMS *Niger* mistook an iceberg for Iceland's North Western Cape. Six merchant vessels followed her into Northern Barrage SN72, a minefield at the entrance to the Denmark Strait. All six struck mines. HMS *Niger* blew up and sank at 22:40. There were only eight survivors out of a crew of 127. The merchant vessels *Hybert*, *Rodina*, *Hefron*, *John Randolph*, and *Massmar* all sank, with only the *Exterminator* being salvaged. 172 souls were lost in this calamity.

Convoy PQ17 sailed from Hvalfjord, Iceland on 27 June bound for Archangel – Murmansk had been badly damaged by the Luftwaffe. On 3 July, QP13 and PQ17 received a warning that the *Tirpitz* was no longer at anchor in northern Norway. The *Tirpitz*, and her sister ship, the *Bismarck*, were the two most powerful vessels in the Kriegsmarine. The Admiralty projected that it was going to attack both PQ17 and QP13. This prospect terrified every soul in each convoy. Tirpitz's eight 15 inch guns and 30 knot capability (35 mph) would wreak havoc.

The Admiralty's warning caused Captain John Egerton Broome, escort group commander for QP13 to issue the order for the destroyers to move to 'Action Stations' and carry out torpedo exercises. This involved them travelling at full speed towards the horizon, and then about-turning simultaneously to be hidden under the smoke which they had created for themselves and the convoy. As it transpired, QP13 was not required to carry out this manoeuvre against the enemy. However, it was a different story for PQ17.

On Saturday 4 July, after receiving order upon order from the Admiralty, throughout the day, PQ17 received a message at 21:23 entitled 'Immediate', which instructed the convoy to disperse and make for a Russian port. At 21:36, the Admiralty, sent out another message 'Most Immediate' commanding the convoy to scatter. What caused disagreement and bad-feeling afterwards was the fact that the Admiralty had asked the escort force to move away from the convoy (and, in their judgment, away from the *Tirpitz*). Therefore, the merchant vessels had to scatter without any protection in their vicinity.

The *Tirpitz* did not appear. However, the Luftwaffe appeared, as did the U-boats. Out of the 35 merchant ships in PQ17, only 11 reached harbour. Twenty-four were lost, along with their 70,000 tons of cargo, which included 400 tanks, 200 planes, and 3,300 vehicles. This demolition of the convoy revealed how difficult it was to get cargo through during the long, bright, days and nights of summer. To make matters even worse, the Germans had broken the British codes. Many in the Royal Navy were horrified that the convoy vessels had been left to the mercy of the Germans. The merchant ships had been mice abandoned to a pounce of hungry cats.[23]

Tirpitz, German battleship

Lifeboats from the American merchant ship *Carlton* which was in PQ17
and torpedoed on 5 July, 1942

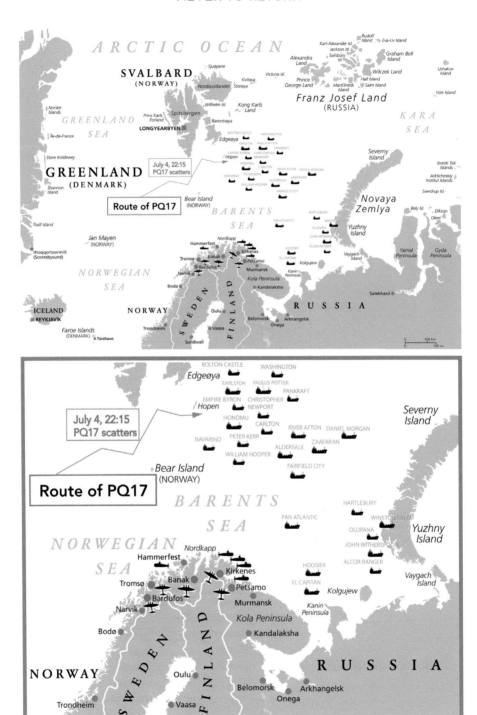

Approximate locations for sinkings in PQ17 which involved the loss
of 24 merchant vessels and one rescue ship, the *Zaafaran*

Cargo ship sunk in PQ17 by U-boat

German reconnaissance picture of PQ17. When PQ17 scattered, U-boats
and the Luftwaffe caused terrible losses

Table of Vessels in PQ 17 and what happened to them

NAME	NATIONALITY	FATE
Alcoa Ranger	United States	Sunk by U-255
Aldersdale	Royal Fleet Auxiliary	Damaged by aircraft Sunk by U-457
Azerbaidjan	Soviet Union	Damaged; reached port safely
Bellingham	United States	Reached port safely
Benjamin Harrison	United States	Reached port safely
Bolton Castle	United Kingdom	Sunk by aircraft
Carlton	United States	Sunk by U-88

Christopher Newport	United States	Damaged by aircraft Sunk by U-457
Daniel Morgan	United States	Damaged by aircraft Sunk by U-88
Donbass	Soviet Union	Reached port safely
Earlston	United Kingdom	Damaged by aircraft Sunk by U-334
El Capitan	Panama	Damaged by aircraft Sunk by U-251
Empire Byron	United Kingdom	Damaged by aircraft Sunk by U-703
Empire Tide	United Kingdom	Reached port safely
Exford	United States	Damaged by ice, turned back
Fairfield City	United States	Sunk by aircraft
Grey Ranger	Royal Fleet Auxiliary	Damaged by ice; reached port safely
Hartlebury	United Kingdom	Sunk by U-355
Honomu	United States	Sunk by U-456
Hoosier	United States	Damaged by aircraft Sunk by U-376
Ironclad	United States	Reached port safely
John Witherspoon	United States	Sunk by U-255
Navarino	United Kingdom	Sunk by aircraft
Ocean Freedom	United Kingdom	Reached port safely
Olopana	United States	Sunk by U-255
Pan Atlantic	United States	Sunk by aircraft
Pan Kraft	United States	Sunk by aircraft
Paulus Potter	Netherlands	Damaged by aircraft. Sunk by U-255
Peter Kerr	United States	Sunk by aircraft
Rathlin	United Kingdom	Reached port safely
Richard Bland	United States	Ran aground, towed back to port
River Afton	United Kingdom	Sunk by U-703
Samuel Chase	United States	Reached port safely
Silver Sword	United States	Reached port safely
Troubador	Panama	Reached port safely
Washington	United States	Sunk by aircraft
West Gotomska	United States	Developed engine trouble, returned to port
William Hooper	United States	Damaged by aircraft Sunk by U-334
Winston-Salem	United States	Ran aground, abandoned and later recovered
Zaafaran	United Kingdom	Sunk by aircraft
Zamalek	United Kingdom	Reached port safely

CHAPTER 8

CONVOY COMMODORES

Amongst the 181 commodores in charge of merchant shipping in ocean convoys (North Atlantic, Arctic, and other areas), there were 11 admirals, 33 vice admirals, 53 rear admirals, and 13 captains. No matter the rank which they had attained before the war, in convoy duty they were all titled Commodores Royal Naval Reserve and were subservient to the Royal Navy's Escort Force Commander. The commodore was supported by his own signal unit from the Royal Navy, usually a signals petty officer (yeoman of signals) and two or three signallers. They would use Aldis lamps, semaphore flags, and telescopes to transmit and receive messages, essential when strict radio silence had to be maintained. Code books were kept in a weighted bag to ensure they sank, if thrown overboard in an emergency.

Seventy-eight convoys sailed to the Arctic between August 1941 and May 1945, a journey which was laden with peril. The distance between Iceland and the ports in North Russia was 2,000 miles in the winter and 2,300 miles in the summer. In the summer, the convoys could follow a safer, but longer course, because the ice would be further north. There was almost 24 hours of continuous daylight in summer and this gave the enemy greater opportunity to attack a convoy. For 1,4000 miles of the journey, there was the danger of air attack; for 2,000 miles of the journey, there was the danger of enemy surface vessel attack; and for every mile of the journey there was the danger of U-boats. Understandably, because of the longer daylight hours, the stress on crews during the summer months was more acute. In winter, twilight conditions prevailed between 08:00 and 15:00 which shortened the period for enemy attack. However, low temperatures reaching down to -20° C, presented separate hardship for the crews.

The burden of convoy protection fell to the Royal Navy. Frequently, there were more Royal Navy vessels in a convoy than merchant vessels and, though the convoy did not see them very often, submarines supported the surface vessels. If the Royal Navy Commander's convoy protection role was challenging, so also was the task of the Convoy Commodore who had to ensure the merchant vessels sailed safely in company, like whales enjoying the collective strength and vigilance the pod affords.

Many of the commodores had retired from the sea before the war commenced. But now, because of the hostilities, they had returned to defend their nation. Most of the commodores had been captains or flag officers in the Royal Navy or Royal Naval Reserve. They had the bearing and sea experience to bring their convoy to port safely and on schedule.

The commodore's ship was placed at the head of the centre column of the convoy, and was identified by a broad white swallow-tail pennant with a blue St George's cross. When a convoy was ready to sail, the commodore gave the order for merchant vessels to take up their respective positions in their columns – a position given beforehand at the onshore meeting.

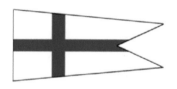

Pennant of Commodore
Royal Naval Reserve

There would then be a vortex of ships circling each other and easing into their column spots. The standard convoy configuration was wide rows and short columns. On leaving the loch or fjord and entering the open sea, the commodore would constantly caution the merchant vessels to maintain the column structure.

The RAF provided air cover for the convoy with land-based aircraft. However, the protection could only extend to the range of the planes. The first few days at sea were normally peaceful for an Arctic convoy, and this gave the Commodore the opportunity to carry out exercises. During the day he would use the ship's steam whistle or signal flags to give out orders. At night, coloured lights would be used. Some of the exercises might include emergency turns, or zig-zagging, or altering course and speed. He would ensure that all ships could carry out the exercises and deal with any challenge which came their way. This was not an easy task in the confusion of war when distress rockets were being fired here and there, when there were distracting loud explosions from detonating depth charges, when huge lumps of water would cover a vessel following enemy shelling or bombing and, as distracting as thunder and lightning, the flashes and sounds of big guns firing.

In addition to the above, the commodore had to plot the convoy's course to Murmansk precisely, and that often under atrocious weather conditions, including disorienting fog and raging seas. Brutal weather could last for days or even weeks. Nevertheless, the convoy would reach harbour at last and in the formation given at the beginning of the journey. The gaps left by ships which had been sunk were closed. The war munitions so badly needed – planes, tanks, lorries, vehicles, ammunition, and oil – were delivered. This delivery was due to the knowledge and experience of the commodores, many of whom died serving Britain and Russia.

Commodore Robin Aveline Melhuish was one of the stalwarts who commanded the merchant vessels of the Arctic Convoys. His story and connection with the sea went back many years to 1900 when he was 14 years of age.[24] He began his instruction on HMS *Worcester*, a timber vessel built in the middle of the 19th century. It served for several years as a training college on the River Mersey.

Commodore Robin Aveline Melhuish

The lecturers on board HMS *Worcester* – the Captain, the officers, and junior officers – were from the Royal Navy and the Merchant Navy. The academic subjects were delivered by civilian teachers. The college comprised six classes with around 30 students per class. The fees were £62.75 for the senior class, and £57.75 for the elementary class. Melhuish was awarded many prizes during the two and a half years he attended. For the navigation prize he received an atlas he could barely lift, so big was it; however, it was crammed with detail which he would devour. He was also awarded a medal from the Royal Meteorological Society in 1900 for the best essay on the meteorology of the Indian Ocean.

HMS *Worcester* had an excellent reputation for instructing students, and several famous individuals received their training there. For example, Admiral Togo and Lieutenant HR Bowers attended as students. Togo won fame in 1905 at the Battle of Tsushima where 21 Russian warships were sunk by the Imperial Japanese Navy. Togo said of his days at HMS *Worcester* that he received instruction there on 'how to behave as an English gentleman.' Lieutenant Bowers perished with Captain Scott on Scott's last expedition to the Arctic in 1912.

After a few years working with British shipping companies, Robin Melhuish went in 1906 to the Royal Indian Marine (RIM) as a sub-lieutenant. The origins of the RIM went back to the 17th century when 'the Honourable Company of the Merchants Trading to the East Indies' was established in 1601 by Royal Charter granted by Queen Elizabeth I. (The adjective 'Honourable' in the title was incongruous according to some because of the company's shady business behaviours.) In the 18th and 19th centuries, however, the RIM was recognized for the excellence of its marine surveying. It was without peer. The RIM carried out surveys between the coast of Africa and the North China Sea and from Suez to Tasmania. The names of RIM officers bedeck the promontories, rivers, bays, inlets, straits, and harbours of the eastern waters.[25]

Melhuish was particularly skilled in survey work and attained the rank of captain in 1931.

He was still in the employ of the RIM when its name was changed to the Royal Indian Navy (RIN). He retired in September 1934, approaching 50 years of age, but was asked to return to the RIN in 1939 and was made Honorary *Aides de Camps* (ADC) to the Ruler of Madras in March 1940. Shortly after this, he left the RIN for a second time and returned home to England.

Back in the United Kingdom, he was informed by 'two men in grey suits' that his services as a convoy commodore were required by the Royal Naval Reserve.

His first role was as vice-commodore on SS *Emma Bakke*. This convoy of 28 ships sailed from Liverpool on 29 May, 1942, bound for Boston. On the voyage, the Queen Mary passed by, sailing on her own to Liverpool. Neither the *Queen Mary* nor the *Queen Elizabeth* ever sailed with a convoy. These vessels were capable of 33 knots (38 mph) and, therefore, were not in the same danger as they would have been in a convoy sailing at 10 knots (12 mph).

'Operation Torch' was the next convoy on which Robin Melhuish sailed. According to reports, this was the biggest armada ever seen. By this time, Melhuish had been promoted to Commodore, and he sailed on SS *Narkunda*, a passenger vessel belonging to the P&O line.

They left the Clyde on 1 November 1942 to deliver soldiers and landing craft to the shores of North Africa. They arrived safely. On the return journey, however, she was sunk after three German attacks. Melhuish and most of the crew survived the sinking.

In December 1942, about a month after the *Narkunda's* sinking, Melhuish was sent to Loch Ewe. He was to be commodore for JW51B, a convoy with 15 merchant ships. The commodore's pennant was raised on the SS *Empire Archer,* a cargo vessel of 7,000 tons. She was carrying 141 lorries, 18 tanks, 21 warplanes, and 4,376 tons of mixed cargo.

For a captain whose experience was in the warm waters of the Indian Ocean, this sea journey to the Arctic was unlike any other journey he had been on. Many of those who have sailed on a Russian convoy say that their most enduring memory is of the atrocious weather met on the voyage – it was a merciless enemy day and night. Surprisingly, it is the Gulf Stream which causes this extreme weather – warmer waters originating in the Caribbean Sea meet the ice and high atmospheric pressure of the Arctic. Because of this, violent gales would arise. Unless the captain altered course to keep the bow of the boat heading into the high waves, the vessel would be swallowed up by the billows. In addition, it was a trying task to keep watch on an open deck in a gale. In the low temperatures of the Arctic, machines would freeze up because of ice clumps of 6" or more. Masts, aerials, and other equipment would be encrusted with the frozen sea water. Guns and torpedo tubes would fail unless the crew kept them ice free. When the gales stopped, there was then the possibility of fog, and vision would be restricted to a few yards. Crews had to be vigilant. If they were not, death might ensue. However, at the meeting in the wooden hut in Loch Ewe prior to JW51B sailing, no one would sense that these challenges were troubling Robin Melhuish.

The Commander of the Escort Force, Captain Robert St Vincent Sherbrook, spoke first at the briefing meeting, explaining to the master mariners, captains of the escort vessels, and to the Commodore and his team the tactics they would use in the event of enemy action. After Sherbrooke's talk, Commodore Melhuish spoke of convoy order and of how each vessel had to maintain its allocated place. He also reminded them not to make smoke without good reason, as its presence would reveal the convoy position to the enemy.

Royal Navy Commander
Robert St Vincent Sherbrooke

At night, they must try to keep as close to the other vessels in the convoy as possible, despite bad weather and magnetic compasses which malfunctioned in such close proximity to the Pole. There was another difficulty the commodores had and this was the type of sailor which might manifest himself on a merchant vessel as a crew member.

Near the end of December 1942 on convoy JW51B, and in the middle of a violent storm in the Barents Sea, a message came to Commodore Melhuish that some of the crew on his ship had broken into a store where rum was being kept for the crew of a minesweeper in the Kola Inlet. A huge brawl was in progress where knives were being used, and sailors were receiving stab wounds. However,

Wooden meeting hut, Loch Ewe

Clearing deck of HMS *Scylla* after severe snowstorm

these stokers were not the normal firemen you would find on a merchant ship. They were from Barlinnie Prison in Glasgow. Authorities faced with a desperate shortage of seamen on this occasion, had offered them one hundred pounds if they would sail on a convoy.[26]

The captain and several crew members from the bridge came down to calm matters, which was no easy matter. In addition to the human chaos, a locomotive had broken its chains, and this huge iron monster was reeling backwards and forwards with each storm-tossing of the ship. Eventually, order was restored for both the animate and inanimate. Melhuish firmly directed each prisoner's attention towards the real enemy, the Germans.[27]

Arnold Melhuish in his book *Commodore Robin Aveline Melhuish* concludes the tale of the Barlinnie firemen after JW51B had reached Murmansk:

The injured firemen (wounds caused in their drunken brawl) were taken by sledge and van through deep snow to a Red Army field hospital, accompanied by Yeoman Matthews…Part of the journey was in an armoured train which was attacked by German ski troops. Matthews was subsequently, Mentioned in Dispatches.[28]

In the five years of war between 1939 and 1945, 4,025 convoys sailed the oceans. One thousand, four hundred and eighty of them crossed the Atlantic; 653 went to Gibraltar; 78 went to the Arctic; and the remainder to places such as North Africa, the South Atlantic, and the Indian Ocean. The Atlantic convoys sailing between America and Britain lost 12.5% of their vessels, and the convoys to Gibraltar 12.5%, but in the Arctic 27% of vessels were lost.

Churchill was correct when he named the Arctic Convoys 'the worst journey in the world'. Three thousand sailors and servicemen lost their lives in them. The Commodores are to be lauded for their leadership in what was known as 'the Murmansk Run'.

CHAPTER 9

CARE AND ASSISTANCE

It is the nature of man, especially at sea, to aid fellow mortals in peril. In the convoys, the acknowledged rule was that the boat at the rear of each column would go to the aid of a sinking vessel.

It is easy to understand why this rule existed, but there was a downside to it. If a fully laden merchant ship stopped, it was itself in danger of being lost. It was easier to fire a torpedo or a shell at a stationary target than at one which was moving. And this frequently happened. And two boats would be sunk instead of one. The result was that some vessels at the rear of columns refused to stop because the danger in doing so was so great. In addition to this, on the return journey from Russia to the United Kingdom ships would usually be without a cargo and in ballast. This meant that the ship's deck would be so far above the water line that it would be difficult to haul survivors aboard.[29] The freeboard was much too high. For these reasons, another system for rescuing sailors had to be found.

In September 1940, Admiral Sir Martin Dunbar-Naismith VC, KCB, KCMG, C-in-C Western Approaches recognised that bespoke rescue vessels had to be found for this work.[30] The Royal Navy did not have rescue ships and, therefore, these would have to come from the Merchant Navy. The first rescue vessels which went to the Arctic were ones which formerly had been sailing around the coast of Britain. They were around 250 feet in length, 1,500 tons in weight, and with a freeboard much lower than the larger vessels. The rescue ship would be located at the rear of a convoy in one of the centre columns, and from this position it could identify vessels which were in difficulty and falling behind the convoy. The rescue vessel would then sail to the stricken ship and provide what assistance they could.

At the beginning, these rescue vessels were berthed at Greenock, and afterwards at Glasgow. The boats came from companies which sailed around the British coast. For example, each one of the 11 Clyde Shipping Company vessels was taken over for this work. Very experienced sea captains commanded them and no rescue ship was lost due to a storm. Convoys usually sailed at 10 knots (12mph) and the rescue vessels could make 11-12 knots (13-14mph). Therefore, it was possible for them to catch up with a convoy after a rescue mission. Initially, because the situation was urgent, not much alteration was made to the 29 boats which had been requisitioned for both Atlantic and Arctic convoy work.

Progressively, additional berths and sanitary facilities for up to 180 men would be installed. Increased washing facilities were required as survivors would often be covered in oil. Carley floats, larger freshwater and fuel tanks would also be fitted. Water tanks would be enlarged by adding an additional shell to the hull of the boat. The normal lifeboats would be replaced by boats more suitable for rescue work. To help survivors board a rescue ship scrambling nets were added and a boom with netting. The boom could be swung out to lift sailors from life rafts. Medical facilities to treat the wounded were installed – a sickbay, an operating theatre, a surgeon, and initially one medical attendant. The upgrading of medical provision was necessary as medical officers would not normally have been part of a merchant ship's crew. Previously, the captain himself would have had to treat sailors who fell ill using the resources available in the ship's medicine chest.

When news got around that there was a Surgeon Lieutenant on the convoy, he would become GP to thousands of sailors. There would be approximately 2,500 sailors on a small convoy and around 10,000 on larger ones. It was customary to move the doctor or the patient from one ship to another whilst at sea to provide medical aid.

The first duty of rescue ships was to take survivors on board when a ship was sunk. They had a ship's boat on either side of the rescue ship so that they could always lower and retrieve on the leeward side. To enable a ship's boat to be launched speedily, mechanical davits with electric winches were fitted to them. The boats were also fitted with powerful engines to enable them to cope in strong seas. Before their installation, crews had to row these skiffs – one can only imagine the exertion and difficulty this entailed.

After an event such as a ship having been torpedoed and sunk, a ship's launch would be dispatched and spend around two hours searching for survivors. Whilst the motor launch was combing the area, the rescue ship herself would be in danger. The Germans did not look on them as hospital ships and would attack.

The boats had another duty and that was 'plane guard'. Aeroplanes such as Hurricanes would accompany the convoy and they would be launched into the air from a CAM ship (Catapult Aircraft Merchant Ship). This was an extremely dangerous role for airmen and these motor launches were extremely efficient in rescuing aircrew when an accident occurred.

Apart from the medical improvements, rescue ships received better signalling equipment. Ten-inch projectors were installed on each side of the bridge to serve as signal lamps and as small searchlights. The radio equipment was upgraded to Royal Navy standards and radio telephone apparatus was also installed.

The rescue ship Copeland

It is reckoned there were around 29-30 rescue ships in total, some being converted trawlers or ocean-going tugboats. They supported 797 convoys and are calculated to have saved 4194 lives.

Six were lost to enemy action, and one sank off the coast of Newfoundland due to ice accretion. These boats were stable in rough seas and the work they did is commendable.

One remarkable story is told of Captain Bill Hartley[31] and his first voyage as master of a rescue ship. He captained the *Copeland* which left Loch Ewe on 2 September, 1942 to provide medical cover for PQ18. PQ18 was one of the largest convoys to sail to Russia and comprised 40 merchant vessels.

At 15:15 on 13 September, a Heinkel HE 111 attacked the merchant vessel *Empire Beaumont*, which subsequently sank at 18:30 that evening. Despite the precarious condition of the *Empire Beaumont*, 68 out of the 74 crew were saved. The *Copeland* rescued 42 of them from the icy waters. Later Captain Hartley and his crew repelled two bombers which had attempted to sink him. Following this, he took on board 163 men whom the escort force had rescued. After receiving medical treatment on the *Copeland*, most of the survivors were transferred to Royal Navy vessels returning to the UK. The condition of hospitals in Russia was so poor that it was not safe for patients to recuperate there.

Five days later, on 18 September, with the *Copeland* and the convoy now nearing Russia, Captain Hartley received an order to pick up an injured American sailor from the merchant vessel *Patrick Henry*.[32] It was too dangerous to stop to carry out the transfer. Therefore, the *Copeland* came alongside the *Patrick Henry*. The two maintained a speed of 9 knots (10mph). The patient was safely transferred and received life-saving medical treatment. (It was not through enemy action, though, that the sailor had been wounded, but through a knife attack by a member of his own crew who had gone berserk because of the repeated enemy air attacks.) When the *Copeland* reached *Archangel*, the survivors were put ashore to recover in more suitable living accommodation. Eighty-seven of them were Russian. Captain Hartly was awarded the DSO for his work on PQ18.

In February 1944, Hartly left the *Copeland* to become master of the *Goodwin*, another rescue ship. In April, he went to the aid of the *South America*, a Norwegian boat. *U-302* had struck her with a torpedo and she had immediately caught fire, with flames rising to the top of her mast. Hartley reckoned that there was only one way to save the crew, and this was to go to the stern of the merchant vessel. When the *Goodwin* was about 70 yards from it, another large explosion took place. A second torpedo had been fired, but surprisingly the blast extinguished the fire on board. The *Goodwin* then sailed to within 40 yards of the *South America* and rescued all the crew within the space of 37 minutes.

Crews

It was common to see men from the Outer and Inner Hebrides crewing the rescue ships. The captain of a vessel wanted the best sailors. He needed skilled and experienced seamen when bad weather hit; when deck work was required; and when the ship's boat had to be launched in a heavy sea.

Sometimes, neighbours from the islands would be together in the Barents Sea, as happened to David Macdonald and Alex Macleod. They lived next door to each other in the township of Lusta, Waternish in the Isle of Skye and had attended school together. Now they were on convoy duty midst the dangers of the Arctic. Alex was on the rescue ship the *Northern Gem* and David was on HMS *Achates*.

Alex Macleod from Waternish, Isle of Skye, was a crew member on the *Northern Gem* and David Macdonald's friend and neighbour.

In addition, Alex had met his own brother William before the *Northern Gem* sailed from Loch Ewe. William was on a tender which supplied fresh water to the convoy merchant vessels.

The most common contract in the Merchant Navy was the one where officers and sailors signed up for a complete voyage i.e. Clyde to Clyde. This meant a sailor on Arctic convoy duty, to fulfill the contract terms, would have to complete both the outward and inward journeys from the United Kingdom to Russia and Russia to the United Kingdom. If his ship went down, his pay ceased on the day the ship was lost.[33]

The firemen were also carefully chosen. You would need to be skilled and strong to keep the boilers stoked with coal at a temperature which would maintain steam. A fireman would also have to have the surge of strength required when the rescue ship had to increase speed immediately to go to the aid of a merchant vessel sinking in the cold waters of the Arctic.

It is interesting to note that the rescue ships rarely altered their crew members through the years of the war. The crews would remain together and sign up for the same boat, sea-journey after sea-journey. The crews on rescue ships were famed for looking after their vessels meticulously.

Before the war there would be around 25 crew on board a rescue ship, but during the war years this rose to around 70. More catering staff were needed, and more trained crew to handle specialised weaponry such as depth charges, 4" deck guns, and anti-aircraft batteries (*Oerliken* and *Bofors* guns included). The rescue ships were known as DEMS (Defensively Equipped Merchant Ships). This is how a crew (about 63-73 personnel) would be made up:

1 Captain
3 Navigating Officers
1 Chief Engineer
3 Engineer Officers
12 – 15 Seamen
12 – 18 Engine room personnel (there would be fewer on a boat which burned oil instead of coal.)
12 Catering staff
3 – 6 Radio Officers
Medical Officer
1 – 2 Medical Ratings
1 Signalling Staff from the Royal Navy
12 DEMS Gunners

The regular crew were given the original accommodation and sleeping quarters which had been installed when the ship was built. There was also an effort made to give additional long-term, comfortable accommodation to those who fulfilled the new roles of medical personnel, gunners and signalling staff. In every rescue ship the crew accommodation was separate from that provided for survivors rescued after a sinking. Survivors' accommodation was more basic. The rationale was that they would not be on board the rescue ship for a lengthy period.

Intriguingly, in a survey which recorded the types of wounds and the manner of death sustained by sailors, it was found that not many badly wounded sailors came on board the rescue ships. The reason for this was that the very seriously wounded would go down with their ship because they would be unable to escape, especially if they were below deck. [34]

Caring for Survivors

When merchant vessels were requisitioned for rescue work, they then belonged to the Admiralty. Accordingly, the boat owners were provided with all that was necessary to run a ship: food, fuel, stores, crew wages, repairs, and compensation for boat use. When survivors came on board, it was the government who paid for their food at the end of the day. [35]

However, the Government did not provide clothing for the seamen who were rescued. Royal Navy rules did not permit the purchase of civilian clothes for naval personnel, nor was it customary for boat owners to buy clothing for their sailors.

If sailors were not rescued by the convoy rescue ship at the time of sinking, their situation would be perilous in an open lifeboat on the Arctic Ocean. Here is an account by a Russian navigation officer who wrote of a rescue ship he encountered with 50 survivors: [36]

I remember it was 13 July, 1942. That day I was asked to fulfill the duties of navigation officer. Our ship was on the outer patrol near Kola Bay – the main base of the Northern Fleet. The weather was extremely good, calm, and sunny. Suddenly there was a telegram cipher on the bridge. Our commander Kondratyev read the telegram, handed it to me, and gave an order to navigate on the set course. The telegram read, 'To the commander of frigate SKR-32. Our submarine K-22 identified a rescue boat [a ship's lifeboat] with sailors in distress [coordinates withheld]. Locate the boat and save the men. Commander of the Fleet.

The given coordinates were about 30 miles to the north of our position, and a little more than three hours later we found the rescue boat full of freezing men. Fifty sailors had spent several days in the Barents Sea. Some were unconscious. We took them aboard, gave them alcohol and dry clothes. On our way back to Polyarnoye base we realised that six of the sailors were Russian, and they told us the story. The rescued survivors were from the British merchant ship 'Bolton Castle' that was part of PQ17 convoy. They had been sunk by air attack on 5 July.

When survivors were lifted from the water, they would only have the clothes they were wearing, whether it was the uniform of an officer from the bridge, or the vest and denim trousers of a fireman working in the heat of the boiler room. And frequently, these clothes would have been spoilt by the oil which poured out of the boat when it sank. Therefore, it was imperative that there was fresh clothing for them.

Fortunately, the British Sailors Society was willing to provide clothing and toiletries because they knew that the government did not provide funds for these items. And in another providence, the British War Relief Society of the USA was willing to cover the costs that the British Sailors Society incurred in aiding the survivors. In addition to helping the British Sailors Society, this American charity delivered 200 changes of clothing and other items to the Royal Navy for Merchant Navy seamen. One hundred outfits were left in Murmansk and 100 in Archangel, under the responsibility of the Senior British Naval Officer (SBNO) in each location.

In a survivor's kit there was underwear, stockings, shoes, trousers, a jumper or a cardigan, a raincoat or an oilskin, a cap, and gloves. The toiletry pack contained a razor and razor blades, soap, toothpaste, and other items. All this would cost around £5 at the time. Another interesting matter was that electric blankets were provided for survivors who would be shivering or benumbed on account of the cold. Furthermore, there were gifts of books, playing cards, darts, dartboards, and draught sets.

Although rescue ships and medical staff did their best to keep survivors alive, it was not always possible to do so. SA Kerslake, in his account of his time on the *Northern Gem*, relates what happened when a rescued sailor passed away: [37]

I would just like to put a word in here about a job of work that was rather unpleasant, but one that had to be done by someone, and I thought that as I was the coxswain, even though only acting, it should be one of my duties. Thus, with one volunteer, Jack Sullivan, it was my job to see that any of the men that we picked up who were dead at the time, or who died later, were prepared for burial at sea. They were treated with respect and care as much as was possible, but with a great deal of haste in many cases, that I will admit, in order to get the job done quickly if the weather was bad, or if other circumstances warranted it. A piece of stout canvas, needle, and twine, and two fire bars [a heavy bar from a grate or a boiler furnace] were all that were needed to complete the task.

When all was finished, the body was placed on a plank of wood, and was then covered with a flag, a White Ensign or the Red Duster of the Merchant Navy; we then reported to the officer of the watch, who in turn would let the CO know, then either he or the first lieutenant would come down to the deck where most of our crew, and those of the dead man's shipmates who could do so, would gather round while the officer read out of the Holy Bible the usual service for burial at sea. When he had finished, the plank would be picked up and one end placed on the ship's rail; the other end would be raised until the body slid over the ship's side and into the sea, feet first, to its eternal rest. The ship which had been stopped for the short time that this had taken would then get on its way as quickly as possible, for while it lay stopped it made a good and easy target for any U-boat in the locality. There were the odd occasions when the senior officer of the escort would not give permission for the ship to be stopped for the purpose of a burial, for it might be too dangerous and not very prudent to do so.

These were sad occasions for everyone who remained behind to carry on the struggle, especially if one was a person with a sentimental nature. I must confess that I was like that, and often thought about the relatives of the ones who had been Discharged Dead, who they were, and how long it would be before they got to know that their husband, father, or sweetheart would not be coming back to them. But I was not a man to dwell on these things for very long – you could not allow yourself to do so, or you could soon lose your nerve and crack up altogether.[38]

The Bravery of the Doctors

There are many accounts of the bravery of Royal Navy doctors and medical personnel who had to be ferried to rescue ships to provide aid. Sometimes this would have to be done in very bad weather conditions and dangerous seas.[39]

In December 1942, in extreme weather conditions, the order was given to Lieutenant Hood, a young surgeon who was 25 years of age on HMS *Obdurate*, to board the rescue ship *Northern Gem* to provide medical aid to sailors who had survived the sinking of their boat. The report written afterwards stated that the *Obdurate* went as close as was prudent to the *Northern Gem*. A rope was tied round Lieutenant Hood and he leapt seven feet down onto the deck of the rescue ship. The sailors on the *Northern Gem* grabbed him and released the rope.

Hood triaged the wounded, allocating them to three categories: the ones who could not be helped; the ones who did not need immediate assistance; and the ones who required immediate attention. Lieutenant Hood injected one sailor with a pain killer which allowed him to spend the remaining hours of his life in a deep, painless sleep. Another had a piece of shrapnel in his head and would require surgery ashore. He was treated. The majority were laid out on a table in the mess room and were operated on there and then. Lieutenant Hood worked through the day and into the night in rolling, dangerous, gale force seas. He received the DSC for his exemplary gallantry.

The bravery of another doctor was recorded in May 1942. Surgeon Lieutenant Ransom Wallace was on HMS *Martin*, a naval escort ship in convoy PQ16.[40] A German bomber attack was in progress when he and a group of sailors received an order to give medical aid to badly wounded sailors on a Russian merchant ship. The Russian vessel was carrying a cargo of explosives and had caught fire.

A rescue launch was to take Ransom Wallace to the Russian ship which had now lost all power and was at a standstill. The rescue launch did not have an engine, and the sailors had to row her. When Ransom Wallace came close to the Russian ship, inexplicably, she started her engines and pulled away from the rescue launch. What a situation for Ransom Wallace and his team to be in – bombs falling, a rescue launch filling with water from the waves which were breaking over it, and a crew rowing hard to try and catch up with a vessel which was steaming away from them.

Somehow or other, they caught up with the merchant ship and Ransom Wallace boarded, accompanied by a medical assistant. They calmed those who were badly wounded and lowered them on Neil Robertson stretchers into the rescue launch which then returned to HMS *Martin* where they received further treatment.

Medical Facilities ashore in the North of Russia

When the convoys to Russia began in August 1941, it was anticipated they would not last for any length of time. Therefore, those in charge did not see a need to provide medical facilities ashore in northern Russia for servicemen or allied civilians. Moreover, the Admiralty was told that Soviet medical facilities were sufficient. This was not true. It was difficult to improve the situation because the Russians did not want help in medical matters. To British medical personnel, the Russians gave the impression of being proud and stubborn people. To add to the difficulty, anyone who wished to work ashore had to acquire a visa, and this took an age. There was no special dispensation for medical staff.

It must also be remembered that the Russians were fighting for their existence. The battle front was only 20 miles from Murmansk. People were dying of starvation and hospitals were experiencing air attacks. The hospitals in Archangel and Murmansk were under pressure and had little equipment. The reports which came from Royal Naval personnel who had the opportunity to visit the hospitals was that the first thing they noticed upon entering was the stink of sepsis.

At this time, the Russians themselves received medical treatment only if it could help them return to the battle front or to another position. The doctors used a simple rule: 'would the injured recover sufficiently to benefit Mother Russia?' Despite this, Russian medical personnel were considered friendly and helpful where they could be, although provision and buildings were poor for the British and allied wounded. It was surmised that the political leaders were the ones preventing improvements. One Royal Navy medical officer wrote that it was pitiful to think that those who were badly wounded would not receive care and would be left to die – whatever nationality they were.

Towards the middle of 1942, the highest ranking British officer in northern Russia sent a warning to the Admiralty that it was imperative a medical unit be sent to Russia, either to Archangel or Murmansk. The prescience of the officer's warning was confirmed shortly afterwards. In June 1942, the PQ17 disaster occurred, and 1600 survivors arrived at Archangel, many of them wounded, and the hospital was overwhelmed. In September, the same situation was repeated when PQ18 was savaged.

Despite the deficiencies ashore in Russia,[41] medical staff did their best to deliver care to the wounded. One person stood out in his efforts to organise midst the chaos. Gillies MacBain was a temporary lieutenant surgeon on the rescue ship *Zamalek*. With 154 survivors on board, they suffered attack after attack as they made their way to Archangel.[42] At one point, the *Zamalek* had to stop to repair a fuel pipe which had burst. This was repaired under enemy bomber attack whilst isolated from the convoy.

She tied up at the pier in Archangel on 11 July and sent 80 survivors ashore. The other 74 were kept on board as there were no hospital beds for them. In the period *Zamalek* was in Archangel enemy air attack was frequent, and food became increasingly scarce. MacBain, the medical officer, was put in charge of matters. He was not alone, but he was the one who created order out of chaos. A senior radio officer named Wolf, who was on the rescue ship *Zaafaran* was made senior administration officer and began to keep administrative records of those who were wounded. He searched out accommodation and also asked the authorities to take over restaurants so that there would be canteens for sailors. The food was poor, but it was better than what local Russians had to eat.

MacBain wanted to work in the hospitals with the Russians, but they would not permit him. He was given permission only to observe what was happening. He was refused authorisation to provide medical supplies and services. There were no X-ray films, and , therefore, no way of obtaining X-rays. There were no antiseptic procedures. There was no pain limitation strategy. As for operations, there were no drugs to administer general anaesthetics to patients. Only local anaesthetics could be given, if available. Infected wounds were common. MacBain received a DSC for his labours.

When senior commanders in London heard of the plight of wounded survivors, a hospital unit was put on board an American ship, but the Russians would not allow the unit to be assembled on shore because no work visas had been issued for this. Two-thirds of the hospital unit returned home and one third remained to provide a hospital in Vaenga, 18 miles from Murmansk. The hospital was in a former barracks.

The hospital in Vaenga was built after communications at the highest level took place between Churchill and Stalin, with Churchill saying in his own pithy manner: "No hospitals. No convoys."[43] The hospital was set up in October 1942 and it continued to operate until July 1945. Surgeon Commander McEwan, who used to work on cruise liners before the war, was the first medical officer in charge. Assisting him was an officer named Robert Dougall, who had joined the Royal Navy in 1942, and who later became a famous BBC television newsreader. He was sent to Russia because he had done a Russian course with the BBC. At the beginning of the war, he was a senior radio presenter, and it was his voice which told the world in September 1939 that Britain was at war with Germany.[44]

Between 1942 and 1945, the hospital treated 149 patients who were wounded in German raids and 470 patients who had contracted diseases.

It was a challenge to maintain the morale of hospital staff, and to this end concerts were arranged as well as games of football. One report stated, not without a little sarcasm, that more staff were injured playing football than were injured by the Germans. Many staff enjoyed skiing, and this also was a cause of several injuries. One dental officer broke his leg on the slopes and had to be sent to Moscow for treatment.

CHAPTER 10

GERMANY AND NORWAY

The Kriegsmarine had coveted ports in Norway since at least the Great War. Between 1914 and 1918 their naval officers had been frustrated time and again as Britain had impeded access to every route out of the North Sea between the Shetland Isles and the coast of Norway by minefields and naval blockade. This strategy had locked U-boats and German warships in their ports, giving them no opportunity to break out into the open Atlantic. German merchant vessels could not sail either which caused food shortages amongst the population. Between the two World Wars, Kriegsmarine officers pondered this problem and concluded that in any future conflict with Britain, Germany must have bases in Norway. This would negate any defensive minefields that Britain could put in place and allow German U-boats and warships to encircle Britain itself.[45]

It was little wonder then when the war began in 1939 that Admiral Rolf Carls, the third highest ranking officer in the Kriegsmarine, pleaded with Commander-in-Chief, Admiral Raeder, that Germany should invade Norway to gain control of its coastline.[46] Raeder concurred. However, it was not until the night of 8-9 April, 1940 that the German military invasion of Norway took place, and for several reasons.

Strategically, a successful invasion of Norway would give Germany ice-free winter harbours as well as access to the North Atlantic. Also, Germany was dependent on iron ore from Sweden for their steel furnaces. The Nazis reckoned they would need 11 million tons of iron ore in the first year of the war to meet their steel requirements for armaments. In the agreeable summer months, the iron ore was carried from the north of Sweden down through the Gulf of Bothnia and across the Baltic to Germany. There were no issues with this route as Britain could not interfere. However, in winter Germany could not use the sea route because of the ice. Instead, the iron ore had to be transported by rail to the Norwegian port of Narvik. From there, German merchant vessels transported it to Germany. Because the German merchant ships sailed in the neutral waters of Norway for almost all of the journey, Britain could not legitimately attack them. It was imperative that Germany seize this port to guarantee the winter delivery of iron ore.

Another imperative for invading Norway was because of Russia attacking Finland on 30 November 1939. News reached Hitler that Britain and France were combining to raise an expeditionary force in Scotland of 57,000 men to assist the Finns. There was only one suitable route for the British and the French to do this, and that was through Norway and Sweden. Hitler realised that if the allies invaded Norway, transportation of iron ore from Sweden to Germany would stop. In addition, Britain and France would have opportunity to advance into Germany from the north, and Hitler certainly did not want to be fighting on another front. The propaganda coup of Germany adding to its empire by occupying Norway was not absent from Hitler's thinking either.

It was because of all of the above that JW51B and other Arctic convoys found themselves being attacked from several Norwegian locations when they sailed to Murmansk and Archangel.

During their occupation of Norway, Germany received invaluable help from a former Norwegian army officer and politician, Major Vidkun Quisling. Quisling had served as Minister for Defence between 1931 and 1933, after which he tried to establish the fascist *Nasjonal Samling* (National Union) along the lines of the Nazi party, but was unsuccessful. However, Hitler made use of him in the Nazi conquest of Norway, establishing him as Prime Minister between February 1942 and 1945. He was executed in October 1945 on charges that he had betrayed his country and had been involved in treason and murder. The term quisling originated in this man, and to this day his surname is used in almost every language as a synonym for a traitor.

CHAPTER 11

HMS *ACHATES* LEAVES GOUROCK

FOR ICELAND

Monday, 21 December, 1942

In the early morning of Monday 21 December, 1942, HMS *Achates'* Confidential Book Officer went ashore to obtain the codes and cyphers that would be used on the voyage. Yesterday, no one knew where their destination would be. Today, after ten hours of paperwork and planning, everything was arranged. This was how the Royal Navy operated in time of war.

The navigator also went ashore. He was Sublieutenant Kenneth Highfield, a young lad who had just completed his apprenticeship with P&O. He was heading towards the Chart Store where he would collect maps and Q-messages. Q-messages were the latest intelligence about safe pathways through British minefields, and – if they could be obtained – pathways through German minefields.

At 09:00, Lieutenant Commander AHT Johns was on the bridge of HMS *Achates*. He looked across to the mountains on the far side of the Clyde. They were still in dark silhouette as the day lightened behind them. Johns moved to the port side of the bridge and looked up at the *Guireag* (Gaelic word for pimple) – the round hill which gave its name to the town. Below on the quay, the dockers were waiting patiently. Commander Johns gave the order to cast off and the ship moved smoothly out of the harbour.

At the weekend, the quay had been chock-a-block with stores: cans of meat, jam, and condensed milk; and butter, flour, tea, and cocoa (or *kai* as the sailors called it). The Provisions Officer in Glasgow had even put turkeys on board for Christmas dinner.

Fuel and munitions had been loaded four weeks previously following operations in Gibraltar. This was Royal Navy practice when a warship returned home. Ship's crew had the opportunity to go on leave after this task. They were now back from leave and ready to escort another convoy.

Although they had permission, not many of the crew went ashore the night before she sailed. It was Sunday evening and the last opportunity they would have to send letters and Christmas cards home. David Macdonald from Waternish in the Isle of Skye was one of those who wrote home that Sunday evening. David was a friendly individual. When he was in school in Waternish, he was awarded a book for being the most popular boy. The crew of the *Achates* would also say that David was a kind, honest lad.

David on his first day of training

David loved nothing better than to work his dog on the croft, help his parents cultivate the land, and assist in their post office in Lusta. David's father ran a taxi service and David often worked on the car when he wasn't working on the roads for the County Council. He was 22 years of age and intelligent enough to work in the radar cabin of the *Achates* along with two other ratings, one from Manchester and the other from London.

His kindly personality can be seen in the letter he wrote to his mother that Sunday evening before the boat sailed.

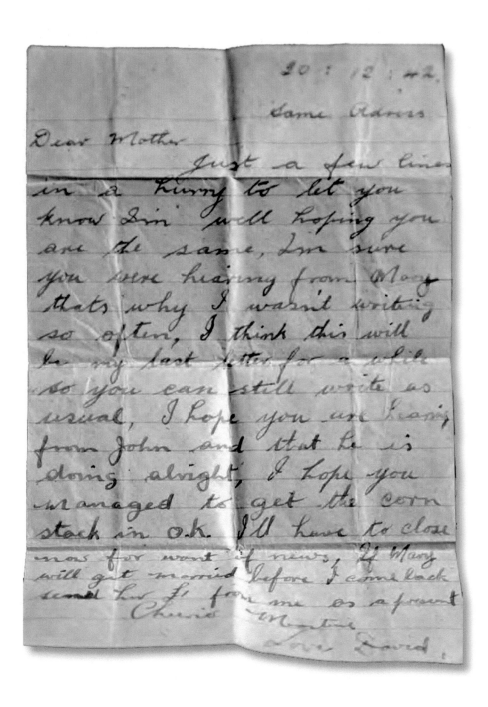

David's last letter

Dear Mother,
Just a few lines in a hurry to let you know I'm well. Hoping you are the same.
I'm sure you were hearing from Mary [David's sister] that's why I wasn't
writing so often. I think this will be my last letter for a while so you can still
write as usual. I hope you are hearing from John [his brother] and that he is
doing all right. I hope you managed to get the corn stack in o.k.
I'll have to close now for want of news. If Mary will get married before I come
back send her £1 from me as a present.
Cheerio meantime.
Love,
David'

There were several who went ashore the night before the *Achates* sailed to have a drink together in a local bar. Amongst them was Lewis man Kenneth MacIver who belonged to Habost, Ness, but was married in North Tolsta. Like many others that evening, he had a foreboding that he might not return. This, most likely, would have had its source in the two previous convoys he sailed in, PQ17 and PQ18, in which many had lost their lives. Here is how George Charlton, another rating on the *Achates* put it:[47]

Having already done two convoys to Russia, I did not relish another. I had leave and told my parents about my forebodings which were that something awful was going to happen, but not to the extent that we were soon to experience. I did not think that we would get away with it three times running. After the hammering we had on PQ18, our luck could not be that good – it must run out sometime.

Kenneth MacIver, on leave in the Isle of Lewis, felt the same. His sense of foreboding was so strong that he left his wife and his young son a day earlier than he had to in order to meet Mary, his wife's sister, in Edinburgh. They had a meal together and then walked to Waverley Station where Kenneth was to get a train to Glasgow and then to Gourock.

Kenneth MacIver

When Mary and Kenneth reached the carriage in Edinburgh, he boarded the train, opened the window, and said to Mary, "I don't know if I am going to come back, but will you make sure you look after the child?" John, Kenneth's son, was one year old.

In the bar in Gourock, sailors from different islands and areas of the United Kingdom were as one. Because Kenneth, at 38 years of age, was a little older than the others, he rose up and said, "This is our last dram together on land. I hope that we will all meet again after this voyage. Here's to Murmansk!" Kenneth used to be in the Seaforths and was well accustomed to proposing a toast. The Seaforths had a tradition – after they had drunk their final dram each would turn towards the hearth and throw his glass into the fireplace. This is what Kenneth did. His friends and he returned to the vessel, brothers in arms, ready to go to Murmansk in the morning.

Not everyone who went ashore visited a pub. First Lieutenant Loftus Peyton Jones, second in command to Commander AHT Johns, had gone ashore before 08:00. He was 24 years of age and belonged to the Channels Islands. His father had been commander of a destroyer in World War One.

That Sunday morning, Peyton Jones and his friend Eric Marland, who was next in seniority to Peyton Jones, had attended church near the top of Guireag hill. They had enjoyed the sermon – its form and message had been like a calm in a storm. As they walked back down the slope, they saw in the Clyde firth ship after ship at anchor, full of every kind of cargo. This convoy had arrived from the far side of the Atlantic on Saturday. It was an encouraging, and yet pitiful sight. The two friends knew that one fifth of the convoy had been sunk, along with one escort destroyer.

Later in the day, Loftus Peyton Jones took the opportunity to go ashore again. He wanted to meet with his girlfriend before he departed. May was in the Wrens and had just finished her shift. Her role was to monitor the signals sent between convoys and the Operations Room. Therefore, she knew how each convoy was faring. They had become acquainted at a dance in the WRENery earlier in the year when he was on PQ16, his first convoy to Russia.

They suited each other – both were kind and compassionate. After the war, Jack Fincham, who was a Chief Petty Officer on the *Achates* wrote about Loftus:[48]

Jimmy the one' was the name the 'lower deck' men referred to the first lieutenant on any ship. He seemed to be a quiet man with a kindly and considerate attitude toward the men and was well-liked. He had all the attributes needed to mould the ship's company into a very efficient fighting unit. Being the senior-ranking officer (although the senior officer, he was most likely the youngest) he was responsible to the captain for the well-being and running of the ship.

On Monday morning, 21 December 1942, all ties to the mainland were cut as HMS *Achates* passed through the boom between Cloch Point and Dunoon. She was following the white wake of HMS *Bulldog*, another naval destroyer assigned to protect convoy JW51B. In a few days, these two vessels would rendezvous in Iceland with other warships and provide the Royal Navy's Ocean Escort Force to Murmansk.

Achates increased her speed. She was now making 18 knots (21mph). There was work to be done en route: the top deck was to be made ready for an ocean voyage; rescue ropes to be prepared; scrambling nets to be secured in anticipation of receiving survivors from other ships; and crew training until each individual was confident he knew what he had to do in an emergency. This work was completed before they passed Ailsa Craig and the question in many minds was: "Would they see the Craig again?"

Further into the journey, Lieutenant Commander Johns requested Lieutenant Peyton Jones and the navigator, Sub-lieutenant Kenneth Highfield, to call upon him in his cabin where he would discuss his sailing orders with them. *Achates* would not be visiting Loch Ewe on the run up to Iceland. "The first thing we have to do," explained Johns, "is to be in Seidisfjord for the 23rd of December. There we shall rendezvous with the other destroyers." The other destroyers were *Oribi*, *Obedient*, *Obdurate*, and *Orwell*. Along with *Achates* and *Bulldog* they made up the 17th Home Fleet Flotilla. Commander Johns continued with his briefing, "Then, after refuelling from the tanker *Scottish American*, we shall meet Convoy JW51B 150 miles east of Iceland." Nine of the merchant ships in JW51B were to sail to Murmansk on the north coast of Russia, and six vessels were to continue to Archangel.

The crew of HMS *Achates* in 1942

CHAPTER 12

CONVOY JW51B SAILS

FROM LOCH EWE

Monday, 22 December 1942

Loch Ewe is in the north-west coast of Scotland and is about 50 miles north of Kyle of Lochalsh and some 80 miles west of Inverness. It was chosen carefully by the Royal Navy as the main military base for convoys following the devastating loss of the battleship HMS *Royal Oak* in Scapa Flow on the night of 13-14 December 1939. On that night, the German submarine *U-47* slipped the defences in Orkney and succeeded in sinking the battleship with the loss of 834 lives.

After the *U-47* attack, the Royal Navy concluded that they had to find a safer anchorage for Merchant Navy and Royal Navy ships. In February1941, Loch Ewe was chosen. As a deep sea loch with unhindered access to the North Atlantic, its location was very suitable: the River Clyde was too far away from Russia and the North Sea; Invergordon and Rosyth were open to air attacks and *U-boat* strikes; and, although Scapa Flow defences were being improved, it was nowhere near being ready.

Loch Ewe was available and very suitable. It provided shelter from westerly gales. It was three miles wide and five miles long – amply large for convoys to use it as a gathering place and anchorage. At the mouth of the loch anti-submarine defences were installed: boom nets, a controlled minefield, and anti-submarine indicator loops.[49]

At 14:15, on the afternoon of Tuesday 22nd December, Convoy JW51B comprising 15 merchant vessels was preparing for the long journey to Murmansk. Their load included 2,046 vehicles, 202 tanks, 87 planes, 33 bombers, 11,500 tons of fuel for motor vehicles, 12,650 tons of aviation fuel, and 54,321 tons of mixed cargo.

Allied Merchant Ships in Convoy JW51B

1.	*Ballot (Panama)*	9.	*Jefferson Myers (US)*
2.	*Calobre (Panama)*	10.	*John H. B. Latrobe (US)*
3.	*Chester Valley (US)*	11.	*Pontfield (UK)*
4.	*Daldorch (UK)*	12.	*Puerto Rican (US)*
5.	*Dover Hill (UK)**	13.	*Ralph Waldo Emerson (US)*
6.	*Empire Archer (UK)*	14.	*Vermont (US)*
7.	*Empire Emerald (UK)*	15.	*Yorkmar (US)*
8.	*Executive Valley (US)*		

*The *Dover Hill* had to withdraw 5 days after leaving Loch Ewe, having been damaged during a Force 12 storm, and suffering boiler trouble. This reduced the convoy to 14 ships.

Close Escort	Ocean Escort
HMS *Bramble*	HMS *Onslow*
HMS *Hyderabad*	HMS *Obedient*
HMS *Rhododendron*	HMS *Obdurate*
HMT *Vizalma*	HMS *Oribi*
HMT *Northern Gem*	HMS *Orwell*
	HMS *Achates*

Cruiser Cover Force	Distant Cover Force
HMS *Jamaica*	HMS *Anson*
HMS *Sheffield*	HMS *Cumberland*
HMS *Matchless*	HMS *Blankney*
HMS *Opportune*	HMS *Chiddingfold*
	HMS *Forester*
	HMS *Icarus*
	HMS *Impulsive*

The weather forecast from the Meteorological Office was for gales accompanied by heavy rain. The gales would hit the west and north-west of Scotland. In Loch Ewe, the anchor chains of the ships were clanking and jangling, and the rigging wires were screeching like banshees. The Meteorological Office forecast was correct.

The hulls of the merchant vessels were painted grey, with splatters of rust here and there. This was not the first time they had been on a convoy. Compared to the slim, narrow naval destroyers beside them, the merchant vessels looked cumbersome and overweight. They had been built to carry cargo and not to race the oceans. JW51B had been designated an eight knot convoy. The fastest merchant ships could deliver only 11 knots (13 mph), and the majority but nine. Perhaps with a little encouragement, engineers could coax a nautical mile or two more out of some of them.

The cracking of the flags in the vicious winds reminded each sailor that it was winter, and that they were going to an even colder location some 2,500 miles distant. Although each flag was grubby with the soot from the funnels ingrained by downpours of rain, it could still be discerned that there were four boats with the red ensign of the British Merchant Navy; nine with the stars and stripes of the United States; one from Panama with two white quarters, a blue quarter and a red quarter; each white quarter contained a star – one blue, the other red.

In addition to the national flag, there was a pennant with two numbers on it. The first number designated the column in the convoy, and the second number the position of the vessel in the column. For example, a pennant with 23 written on it indicated that the boat was in the second column of the convoy and in the third position.

The convoy vessels weighed anchor around 14:45. The weather had moderated a little. One after the other, the ships left Loch Ewe heavy with their cargoes. They passed through the boom gate in a line which stretched for over two miles. The merchantmen started in single file, then gradually formed up into a four column convoy sailing NNW at about 8 knots with their escort. They sailed with the red brick lighthouse of the Butt of Lewis to port, and Cape Wrath, the most north-westerly point in Great Britain, to starboard.

Leaving the Minch behind and meeting the open ocean, the indications were not encouraging. Dark clouds were gathering. A swelling sea was marching in from the west. The turbulent ocean was growling and spitting the spindrift from the wave tops. The snell wind from Greenland's ice-covered mountains was strengthening. JW51B had only just begun its voyage to Murmansk many miles away.

The Western Escort Group Destroyers *Blankney*, *Chiddingford*, *Ledbury* and the minesweeper *Circe* were to accompany the merchant vessels from Loch Ewe to the sea west of Iceland and then return to Scotland. They would be replaced by close escort ships which would protect the convoy all the way to Murmansk. The close escort comprised the corvettes *Hyderabad* and *Rhododendron*, the mine sweeper *Bramble*, and the converted trawlers *Vizalma* and *Northern Gem*. The destroyers *Obedient*, *Oribi*, *Orwell* and *Obdurate* were at this time taking on fuel at Seidisfjord, whilst *Achates* and *Bulldog* were still en route to Iceland. In a short while the 17th Destroyer Flotilla would be gathered 150 miles to the east of Iceland, ready to protect JW51B to Russia. The Senior Officer and overall escort commander, Captain Sherbrooke, was on HMS *Onslow*.

At 13:00, an hour and three-quarters before the convoy sailed, Robin Aveline Melhuish had boarded SS *Empire Archer*, the ship of Captain Maugham. Melhuish was commodore of the 15 merchant vessels in convoy JW51B and the *Empire Archer* was now the convoy flagship because the Commodore and his support team were on it.

Prior to 13:00, Melhuish had attended a conference ashore in a wooden hut, along with Captain Robert St Vincent Sherbrooke. Sherbrooke had received a coded teleprinter communication from Admiral Tovey the day before:

```
CONVOY JW51B 16 SHIPS. SAIL FROM LOCH EWE
22ND DECEMBER. SPEED OF ADVANCE 7 1/2
KNOTS ROUTED AS FOLLOWS... ESCORT LOCH EWE,
HMS BRAMBLE (S.O. M/S FLOTILLA) BLANKNEY,
LEDBURY, CHIDDINGFOLD, RHODODENDRON,
HONEYSUCKLE, NORTHERN GEM, VIZALMA.

CONFERENCE A.M. 22ND DECEMBER WHICH CAPTAIN
D17 [CAPTAIN SHERBROOKE] WILL ALSO ATTEND,
SUBSEQUENTLY PROCEEDING INDEPENDENTLY IN
HMS ONSLOW TO SEIDISFJORD. ORIBI, OBEDIENT,
OBDURATE, ORWELL, BULLDOG, ACHATES, TO
ARRIVE SEIDISFJORD P.M. 23RD DECEMBER.

CAPTAIN D17 IS TO SAIL WITH THESE
DESTROYERS TO JOIN CONVOY IN POSITION C.
WHEN DESTROYERS JOIN, HUNTS [I.E. 'HUNT'
CLASS DESTROYERS BLANKNEY, LEDBURY, AND
CHIDDINGFOLD] ARE TO REMAIN WITH CONVOY TO
PRUDENT LIMIT OF ENDURANCE AND THEN RETURN
TO SEIDISFJORD...
```

Commodore Melhuish spoke after Sherbrooke. He informed each merchant captain which position their vessel would have in the convoy. Route Green was the name given to the course JW51B was to take to Murmansk; most of it would be above the Arctic Circle. Melhuish provided the seven waypoints for the journey. They ran from A to H. The waypoints would take them north of Scotland, up to Iceland, across to the Greenland Sea and then to the Barents Sea. After this they would sail south and enter the Kola Inlet towards Murmansk. Murmansk was the only port in the west of Russia which was free of ice all the year round.

The Russians hoped that the convoy would reach Murmansk safely early in the New Year. That is, if the winter gales did not hamper it, nor the German air attacks, nor the Kriegsmarine surface ship attacks, nor the U-boat torpedoes. The Russians badly needed the cargo of motor vehicles, tanks, and warplanes and bombers in wooden crates; fuel for vehicles and planes; and general cargo (food and other necessary items).

The severe winter storms would bring swelling seas, and waves smacking of the dark Cuillin peaks of Skye. Although it was possible for cruisers to travel as fast as 32 knots (37mph), great seas like this would impede them. They would have to limit their 75,000hp engines to 8 knots (9mph). The waves could toss a 10,000 ton cruiser more easily than an athlete could a caber at the Portree Games. The winds could scatter a convoy like chaff. Normally, the journey to Murmansk would take between 10-12 days, but with storms and enemy attacks the journey could take days extra.

At the end of the meeting, Sherbrooke and Melhuish were satisfied that they had fulfilled their duties. They had communicated official orders for the convoy and outlined the stratagem in the case of enemy attack. However, there was one person in the wooden hut in Loch Ewe who was not satisfied – he was Captain A.V. Radcliffe, RNR, Naval Control Service Officer.

Although he had received assurances from the Admiralty that each vessel which entered Loch Ewe for convoy JW51B would arrive equipped to undertake the journey, this was not the way it had transpired. Boats arrived requiring repairs and stores. Every ship had to be serviced, apart from two. For example, the Executive had damaged deck cargo and required vegetables and 65 tons of water. The Ralph Waldo Emerson needed 150 tons of water along with repairs to her compasses and echo sounder. And, Dover Hill had crew and engine problems. All these requests depleted his resources. But, as usual, Captain Radcliffe had fixed everything before the convoy sailed at 14:15 on Tuesday evening.

Sherbrooke's orders commanded that he make for Seidisfjord with all speed in the *Onslow*. Therefore, he went ahead of the convoy to meet up with the other destroyers in the 17th Flotilla who were waiting for him in Iceland.

He also knew that sleep deprivation was one of the biggest enemies his crew could face, and he wanted to reach Seidisfjord timeously so that they could get a good night's sleep on the 23rd. This is why the Onslow went through the North Minch at 25 knots (29mph). But, the glass was falling and it was not long before the wind was blowing at 50 knots (58mph) – storm force 10.

Onslow ploughed on, maintaining speed. Her bow plunged into the troughs of the waves and emerged like a huge whale, its mouth baling brine. Sherbrooke and his navigator were constantly on lookout to ensure their speed suited sea conditions.

CHAPTER 13

HMS *ACHATES* IN A GALE

Wednesday, 23 December, 1942

The next day, Wednesday, at 05:00 the wind had risen to Force 11, a violent storm. With gusts reaching 55 knots (63mph) and beyond, *Onslow* was in danger of breaking her hull. Sherbrooke had to reduce speed from 25 knots (29mph) to 20 knots (23mph); this was not only for the safety of the boat, but for the sailors down below. They would be thrown about each time the ship fell into a trough. Sherbrooke succeeded in reaching Seidisfjord without heaving to. He had avoided the worst of the gale. It did not go so well for *Achates* or *Bulldog*, who were now 24 hours behind schedule. This is how Loftus Peyton Jones described the journey on HMS *Achates* on 22nd December: [50]

The wind rose steadily during the night and by the time I took over the morning watch at 04:00 on the 22nd the ship was rolling heavily in a quartering sea. We were stationed about a mile abeam of Bulldog, still making a good sixteen knots (18mph), but beginning to yaw rather widely. When the Captain appeared a couple of hours later, it was clear that we should have to reduce speed and Bulldog's signal to come down to twelve knots (14mph) was gratefully acknowledged. All that day we ploughed on under a grey, lowering sky, doing little except to try to keep ourselves warm and dry.

On deck, it was sometimes hard to recognise who was who, muffled up as we were with scarves, balaclava helmets and a great variety of headgear. Layers of sweaters over woollen shirts and long-johns, beneath duffel coats or oilskins, made for somewhat cumbersome movement and just getting about the ship as she corkscrewed through the heavy seas was quite an effort in itself. Green waters swept over the foc'sle and, cascading against the superstructure, sent showers of freezing spray across the bridge. Passage from fo'd to aft along the iron deck became more and more hazardous, even with the help of hanging strops which ran along the wire jackstays rigged on either side, and eventually had to be forbidden altogether, thus effectively separating one end of the ship from the other.

Below deck, sailors were rocking from side to side in their hammocks. The heat was at a comfortable enough temperature due to the steam-heated system, but now and again spurts of seawater would enter the sleeping area through hatches and air vents which were supposed to be watertight. In the engine room and boiler room, the sailors had to move carefully; however, they were warm and being low down in the middle of the boat, they did not experience the twisting and turning of the destroyer as much as those in the bow or stern of the ship.

The weather deteriorated further. Finally, they had to heave to and keep the bow facing into the wind. Both *Achates* and *Bulldog* were now stopped and would not reach Iceland at the time scheduled. Peyton Jones described affairs on the 23rd:

…the next morning found us hove to just riding out the storm, all hope of passage making was abandoned for the time being. By then, the wind had increased to Force 12 (78mph) and the seas risen to a height which I had never seen before – nor ever have done since. Sometimes it seemed impossible for the ship to climb the oncoming wave and one had to hang on tight as the bow rose steeply into the air, but somehow the sharp flared foc'sle would force its way through to the other side and the stern would go up like a lift as the bows plunged down into the next trough.

But it was *Bulldog* and not *Achates* which suffered most. Heavy seas had hit her repeatedly, smashing her ship's boats into smithereens; some of her guns had been damaged, and the ASDIC dome had been flooded. After 24 hours of trying to keep her nose to the wind, *Bulldog's* captain was signalling:

```
Hove to in position 180 degrees, Stokness Light
[Iceland] 8 miles,

Achates in company. Southerly gale, force 12...
```

Force 12 meant that the windspeed was greater than 64 knots (74mph). The outcome was that *Bulldog* had to return to Gourock for repairs because of the damage she had sustained. *Achates* lost her topmast, but this was repaired when she reached Seidisfjord. However, there was more to the *Bulldog's* story. *Bulldog* had hove to as had the *Achates*, but the *Bulldog's* commander thought the wind was softening and had decided to continue onwards. Bulldog's First Lieutenant and Navigator had both tried to give guidance to the young commander who was not familiar with the boat nor this area of the Atlantic. They had advised him that to press on to Seidisfjord in these conditions would cause him to meet an even more turbulent sea. The Captain did not listen and increased speed. This is how Eric Rhead, the navigator, recorded events:[51]

> *The inevitable happened and Bulldog charged into the gale… Most small ships have a breakwater on the forecastle as they normally ship a lot of water in bad weather at speed, and the breakwater just guides the water sideways back into the ocean. In our case the sea was too big, the speed too fast, with the result that the breakwater was just swept back, taking some five feet of the forecastle deck with it, rather like opening a sardine tin. The crew's quarters were swamped and indeed the ship was unsafe…*

The number of destroyers which were left to protect Convoy JW51B was now down to six, and all on account of one tyro who did not heed the advice of experienced officers.

CHAPTER 14

HOW CONVOY JW51B WAS NAMED

There were two convoys to Russia named JW51 – JW51A and JW51B. There was a strategic reason for naming the convoys in this way. The convoys to Russia began in August 1941 as a result of discussions involving Churchill, Stalin, and Roosevelt. Roosevelt and Churchill knew that Stalin had to maintain the conflict with the Germans in the east so that Hitler could not use these military resources in the west.

On the 14th of August, 1941 Roosevelt and Churchill wrote this letter to Stalin:[52]

We have taken the opportunity afforded by the consideration of the report of Mr Harry Hopkins on his return from Moscow to consult together as to how best our two countries can help your country in the splendid defense that you are putting up against the Nazi attack. We are at the moment cooperating to provide you with the very maximum of supplies that you most urgently need. Already many shiploads have left our shores and more will leave in the immediate future....

We realize fully how vitally important to the defeat of Hitlerism is the brave and steadfast resistance of the Soviet Union and we feel therefore that we must not in any circumstances fail to act quickly and immediately in this matter of planning the program for the future allocation of our joint resources.

Franklin D. ROOSEVELT
Winston S. CHURCHILL

However, almost a year later, after the devastating losses suffered by PQ17 in July 1942, Churchill was writing to Stalin to advise to wait for the winter when there would be more hours of darkness, before he sent another convoy. Summer in the Arctic consisted of almost continuous daylight with practically no hours of darkness; this aided the Germans in their attacks on the convoys. The destruction of PQ17 lasted for over a week and out of a total of 35 merchants ships, only 11 arrived at their Russian port. One hundred and fifty-three sailors were lost.

After PQ17, Churchill himself wrote to Stalin on the 17th of August, 1942 saying:[53]

My naval advisers tell me that if they had the handling of the German naval surface, submarine and air forces, in present circumstances, they would guarantee the complete destruction of any convoy to North Russia…it is therefore with the greatest regret that we have reached the conclusion that to attempt to run the next convoy PQ18 would bring no benefit to you and would involve only dead loss to the common cause.

Stalin did not like this at all and wrote:[54]

Our naval experts consider the reasons put forward by the British naval experts to justify the cessation of convoys to the northern ports of the USSR wholly unconvincing. They are of the opinion that with goodwill and readiness to fulfill the contracted obligations these contracted obligations could be regularly undertaken and heavy losses inflicted on the enemy.

After the war Churchill wrote in his book *The Second World War*:

I did not think it worthwhile to argue out all this with the Soviet Government, who had been willing until they themselves were attacked to see us totally destroyed and share the booty with Hitler, and who even in our common struggle could hardly spare a word of sympathy for the heavy British and American losses incurred in trying to send them aid.

However, Churchill was a practical man and he understood that Russia needed the supplies. After meeting Stalin in Moscow in August 1942, and with pressure from Roosevelt, Churchill gave permission for PQ18 to sail from Loch Ewe on the 2nd of September, 1942.

Between 12-21 September the Germans attacked PQ18 with bombs, torpedo bombs, U-boats, and mines. They succeeded in sinking 13 vessels out of the 44 which left Loch Ewe. Convoy PQ18 arrived in Archangel on the 21st of September, 1942. It was obvious that it was becoming increasingly difficult to guard the larger convoys. As a solution, a philosophy emerged which considered it would be safer to send smaller convoys. Instead of 30 vessels being in PQ19, the authorities chose to split them into two convoys, renaming them – JW51A and JW51B. JW51A sailed with 16 merchant ships on the 16th of December, 1942 and on the 25th of December, by good fortune and good weather, arrived in Murmansk without seeing a single German and without a single loss.

However, matters did not go so well for convoy JW51B. They had a very uncomfortable journey from the Minch to the rendezvous point 150 miles off the Icelandic coast. Weather conditions had been extreme. The suffering of the merchant navymen would possibly have been much worse than that of the men of the Royal Navy. The merchant navy vessels were rotund and heavily laden, sitting in the water like a herd of hippopotamuses. If the journey to Iceland had been bad, the days following the rendezvous off Iceland on 25th December were no better. According to the Commodore, the weather deteriorated rapidly on 27th December, blowing a gale from the north-west. In addition to the rocking they received in the heavy seas, there was torrential rain and gale force winds hitting them from behind. On board *SS Empire Archer*, smoke and soot from the funnel was gusting from stern to stem. It was reckoned that the high amount of smoke pouring from the funnel was due to poor coal. Len Matthews, the Commodore's Yeoman on *Empire Archer*, recorded that the smoke 'made us all look like chimney sweeps' and had reduced visibility ahead to almost zero. Robin Melhuish's report mentioned that:

The convoy was considerably scattered by the following morning, but all except one eventually rejoined, although HMS Oribi lost the convoy due to complete compass failure and never found JW51B again. She eventually turned up at Murmansk on her own. [55]

CHAPTER 15

RENDEZVOUS WITH CONVOY JW51B

Thursday, 24 December, 1942

The *Achates* reached Seidisfjord at 11:30 on Thursday, 24th December, and visited the 'oiler', *Scottish American,* to replenish her fuel tanks before anchoring at the head of the inlet which was now becoming congested. She was now in the company of the five other destroyers of the 17th Flotilla. It was an opportunity for the crew of the *Achates* to dry their clothes and make repairs to the boat. Whilst these tasks were taking place, Captain Tyndale Johns went across to the *Onslow* where other commanders were gathering and discussing plans for the journey to Murmansk.

Peyton Jones remained on the *Achates*. He received a visit from the First Lieutenant on the *Onslow*, Lewis King, and he records later that Lewis King had come to ask for some of the sweets and dainties that had been loaded on to the *Achates* on the Clyde, as his ship was going to eat their Christmas meal that night. King received a goodly portion, but Peyton Jones ensured that there was sufficient remaining for the crew of the *Achates* to celebrate with when they reached Murmansk. There had been a vote on the *Achates* and the sailors had chosen to wait until they reached port in Russia. There was general agreement that they would enjoy Christmas dinner better once the strain and stress of the journey was past. And they were so tired and wet that it was bed and a few hours sleep that everyone wanted before they sailed later that evening.

Captain Sherbrooke, the senior officer in charge of the destroyers, sailed at 23:00. He was to meet JW51B about 150 miles off the coast of Iceland the next day, Christmas day. At 23:20 the *Onslow* and the other destroyers were through the boom and into the open sea. The five warships were in one line or 'following 'father' as the sailors called it. The wind had settled and the northern lights were dancing merrily in the Arctic night.

Sherbrooke wore his duffle coat, scarf, and cap whilst on the bridge. Beside him was Lieutenant Peter Wyatt, the navigator, and another officer who was keeping watch. It was always difficult to keep watch at night. Apart from feeling tired, it was challenging trying to see other boats. According to the regulations, each vessel had to keep three cables (a cable in the Royal Navy is one-tenth of a nautical mile, which is 185 metres) from the one ahead of them. In the darkness, the stern of the boat in front was like a black snail. The white wake of the boat ahead was a little help.

Shortly after midnight, a signal came from Admiral Tovey, Commander of the Home Fleet:

> I estimate the position of main body JW51B at 08:00 25th based on an escort aircraft report as 065°14'N, 008°31'W, speed 7 knots. One or two groups of stragglers about 15 miles astern overtaking.

To make certain that they would not fail to meet the convoy, Sherbrooke and the destroyers of the 17th Flotilla sailed beyond where JW51B was reckoned to be. Then, they turned back to face the convoy. The convoy would be but a speck in the ocean. In the foggy conditions, Sherbrooke and the Flotilla could only see three miles in front of them. Because of this, he positioned the five warships in a row, three miles distant from each other; thus extending the arc for watch keeping. This made a line which extended 15 miles and created a 21 mile arc for watch keeping.

There was a system for keeping watch on warships. A number of sailors would be designated for watch keeping, and each individual would have a specific watch arc to cover to observe the ocean closely. Officers on watch on the bridge would not receive an arc. They had to scrutinise the sea in front of them. Fortunately, the sun was behind JW51B and it would outline the convoy to Sherbrooke's advancing flotilla. However, it would be difficult to catch a glimpse of them. As far north as they were, the sun would rise only one degree above the horizon at midday, and there would be a measure of daylight for only five hours between 11:00 and 16:00.

Friday, 25 December, 1942

At 14:30 on Christmas day, a sailor on watch in Sherbrooke's Flotilla spotted the convoy of 13 boats to the south-west. JW51B was sailing north at 8 knots

(9mph). Signal lamps started communicating and Sherbrooke gave the 17th Flotilla the order to alter course to the southwest. They joined convoy JW51B 150 miles north-east of Iceland. To protect the merchant vessels, Sherbrooke in the *Onslow* took up position ahead of Commodore Melhuish in the *Empire Archer*. He positioned the destroyers *Orwell* and *Oribi* to the port side of the merchant group and *Achates* to the rear on the port side. He placed *Obedient* and *Obdurate* to starboard.

At the rear of the convoy, were HMS *Rhododendron*, HMT *Northern Gem*, and HMT *Vizalma*. They were there to deal with U-boat threats and also to provide assistance if any of the vessels were struck by torpedoes. HMS *Bramble* and HMS *Hyderabad* who had the latest and much improved radar sets were sent ahead of the convoy group as pickets to provide warning of enemy activity.

There were also two other vessels at sea, the battleship *Anson* and the cruiser *Cumberland*. They were to provide cover up to Bjørnøya (Bear Island) which was about 1,000 miles away. After Bjørnøya, the cruisers *Sheffield* and *Jamaica* would take over; they were at present in the Kola Inlet near Murmansk. In addition to these ships, there were British and allied submarines patrolling the west and north coast of Norway. Their task was to counter the threats from German heavy cruisers anchored at Altenfjord, Narvik, and Trondheim.

The destroyers HMS *Blankney*, HMS *Ledbury* and HMS *Chiddingfold* were now to leave the convoy according to Admiral Tovey's order of 19 December:

```
After leaving convoy, HMS Blankney return Scapa
for repairs to compass, HMS Ledbury and HMS
Chiddingfold to Loch Ewe.
```

The above three destroyers had accompanied the convoy since it had left Loch Ewe on 22 December. The customary 'Good Luck' signals were exchanged between the remaining and departing naval vessels. The 14 convoy vessels were now under the guardianship of the 17th Flotilla led by Captain Sherbrooke. Slowly but surely, JW51B sailed north at 8 knots. The Royal Navy escort vessels were back and forth like hens watching over their chickens, their ASDICs pinging listening for any German activity below the surface. Tired eyes were also scanning sky and ocean for Luftwaffe and Kriegsmarine.

Unknown to the convoy, a German spotter plane had observed it on the day before Christmas. This was the reason that Kapitänleutnant Herbschleb was stalking in *U-354*. Herschleb wrote in his diary that there was a bright, silvery moon that Arctic night (24 December) which clearly revealed the ships in the convoy.

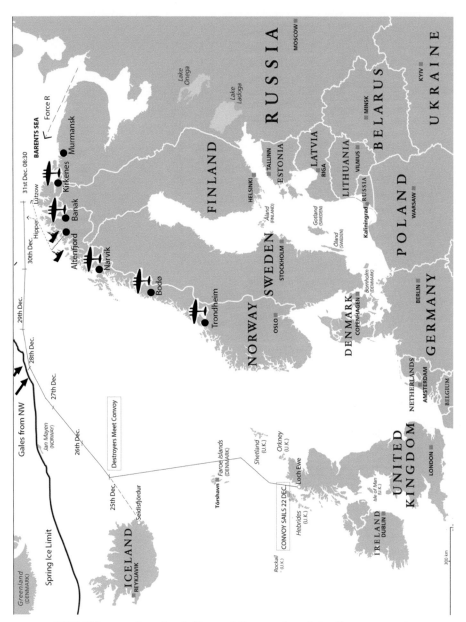

JW51B's route from Loch Ewe to Murmansk and the German attack
on 31st December 1942

Short Sunderland S25 on convoy duty

However, not every plane which spotted the convoy was an enemy. On Christmas day, a Liberator, a long-range bomber, from Coastal Command saw the convoy. When it glided past the *Onslow* like a huge seabird, a sailor sent a message by signal-lamp providing latitude and longitude and speed of the convoy. JW51B was following a course to the north-west of 320° at a speed of 8.5 knots. The sextant reading at noon that day was 68° north. The convoy was now inside the Arctic Circle.

When the Liberator returned to Iceland, the information about the convoy was transmitted to the Admiralty in London. Therefore, Commander Robert Sherbrooke did not have to break radio silence. This was important because he would use the radio in an emergency only – if they saw a German vessel, for example. If there was a need for convoy ships to communicate by radio they would do so but at very low power so that the enemy would not pick up the transmission. Even at this, a U-boat could pick up the signal if it was close by. However, enemy headquarters in Norway would not be able to pick up these low-power radio transmissions. Shortly after the Liberator departed, a Catalina flying boat appeared. This too circled the convoy, observing its steady progress.

However, one thing was disturbing Commodore Melhuish: the SS *Empire Archer*'s funnel was smoking badly. She burnt coal and her funnel was low. With the wind direction coming from the rear of the boat and blowing towards the bow, the bridge was engulfed. Those on the bridge were coughing and their eyes were streaming. They could not see in front of them. But, worse than these things, there was the grave risk that the smoking funnel would betray the convoy position to the enemy. Smoke could be discerned from much further away than the outline of a ship.

The air temperature had decreased greatly when the convoy crossed the Arctic Circle. However, despite the cold and the hardship, the ships' crews were keeping up their spirits. On the bridge of the *Empire Archer*, a sailor called Matthews smoked a cigar for his Christmas treat. Surely his thoughts would be on his home in Britain. And surely his family would be remembering him, though in all likelihood, they would not know he was on the Murmansk run.

CHAPTER 16

BEYOND THE ARCTIC CIRCLE

Saturday, 26 December 1942

At midday on the 26th of December, the convoy was at coordinates 68°23'N, 6°32'W and still sailing north. Because they had crossed the Arctic Circle the hours of daylight were reduced. Despite gloves and mittens, seaboots and woollen stockings to try and thwart the increased coldness, it was difficult not to become benumbed midway through a four-hour-long watch. And, after completing a watch, it would take some time before hands and feet recovered sufficiently to allow sailors to sit down to eat or to stretch out on their bunk.

Two days into the voyage and the crew were already feeling fatigued. Captains and navigators also had to snatch sleep whenever they could. It was rare for them to leave the bridge.

They knew that they were but starting 'the most dangerous journey in the world' as Churchill named it, and that it would take around another nine days to reach Murmansk.

Apart from a mine spotted by Commodore Melhuish, and which was sunk by the *Rhododendron,* Boxing Day was quiet.

Convoy JW51B's position at 12:00 on 26 December, 1942

Sunday, 27 December 1942

At midday, Convoy JW51B was now at coordinates 70°48'N 00°22'W and travelling at 8 knots. The sea state was calm but deadly cold.[56] The further north the convoy sailed, the less daylight they had – perhaps two to three hours of daylight after midday. The dusky light quality was akin to the close of a winter day in the Isle of Lewis or the Isle of Skye.

On this day also, Admiral Burnett sailed with *Force R* from the Kola Inlet to provide distant cover for JW51B. The plan was to be within 50 miles proximity of JW51B by the 29th of December. Burnett was on the cruiser HMS *Sheffield*. With *Sheffield* was HMS *Jamaica*, another cruiser, and HMS *Musketeer* and HMS *Matchless*, both destroyers. The Germans noticed that *Force R* had left the Kola Inlet. However, once Burnett and his group were in the Barents Sea, spotter planes were unable to locate it.

Admiral Oskar Kummetz in the heavy cruiser *Admiral Hipper* believed *Force R* had left harbour to protect convoy JW51A, which had now been renamed RA51. However, RA 51 was still in the Kola Inlet and preparing to return home on 30 December. JW51A had a favourable outward journey with all 16 convoy merchant vessels arriving in Murmansk safely, having left Loch Ewe

Convoy JW51B's position at 12.00 on 27 December, 1942

Admiral Oscar Kummetz

on 15 December. Kummetz's assessment was correct up to a point, because Force R was going to provide cover for convoys JW51B and RA51 at the same time, but would assist JW51B first.

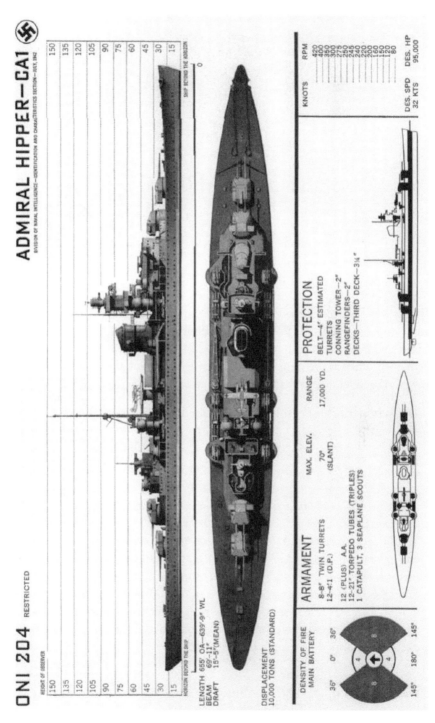

Admiral Hipper recognition drawing

CHAPTER 17

STORM AND ICE

Monday 28 to Tuesday 29 December, 1942

Midday was the Royal Navy's scheduled time for calculating vessel positions, and on the 28th at 12:00 JW51B was reckoned to be at 72°35'N and 4°20'E and on a course of 071°. The wind had risen to force 7 (28-33 knots) from the north-west. Ice was forming on ships' rigging and great swells were tossing the convoy to such an extent that they had to reduce speed to 6.5 knots.

This is how Loftus Peyton Jones described the journey to date:[57]

We enjoyed two days of reasonable weather before the wind started to rise once more. By the morning of Monday 28th it was blowing a good Force 7 from the west and steering and station keeping became very difficult. Achates rolled heavily in the quartering seas and as the spray came aboard it froze on superstructure, guns, decks and guardrails. We felt even sorrier for the smaller corvettes and trawlers whose decks were continually swept by green and greedy seas. All through those hours of twilight that passed for daytime, snowstorms swept across the convoy and visibility was often less than a cable. Station keeping became a real nightmare and not a few near collisions resulted as ships did their best to stay in some sort of formation. The strain of bridge watchkeeping under those conditions was the worst I have ever experienced and the only consoling thought was that the enemy must be suffering an equal degree of discomfort.

On the night of the 28th and into the morning of the 29th, strong gales pummelled them again. This time the venomous wind was blowing north north-west and the gyration for ships was worse. The *Jefferson Myers* had to heave to when her deck cargo shifted. Commodore Melhuish was not amused and he said afterwards that the *Jefferson Myers* did not have to stop and lose her place in the convoy. He surmised that the problem was poor loading of cargo. On the morning of the 29th, the deck cargo of the *Daldroch* moved as well.

From 01:00 to midday those on watch could not, at times, see more than 600m ahead of them. At midday the convoy coordinates were 73°19'N 11°45'E. In the afternoon the wind had fallen and the lookouts could now see 10 miles ahead of them (18km), but there were only nine ships visible and they were out of their convoy formation. There was no sign of HMT *Vizalma* or the destroyer *Oribi*. Because *Bramble's* radar was more advanced than most of the other escort ships, she was sent to seek out the strays – the lost sheep as it were. JW51B's speed was reduced to 6 knots to enable those who had lost contact to catch up with the convoy.

Peyton Jones relates that when they made a roll call, nearly one third of the convoy was missing. And, the nine vessels which did respond to the roll call were scattered across a large portion of the ocean. It was the task of the escort ships to gather them in again. *Oribi* was missing also and later the captain reported that his gyro-compass had failed. She had to sail by herself to Murmansk, keeping closer to Norwegian coastland than she would have wanted. The convoy was now without an important escort destroyer.

Over the last few days, tons of ice had gathered on the decks and on the ship's equipment and superstructure. On the *Achates'* guard rail, the ice was as thick as a man's arm. Peyton Jones commented:[58]

With all this additional top-weight the ship rolled sluggishly and until the guns, torpedo tubes, and depth-charge throwers could be freed we were clearly not an efficient fighting unit. Fortunately, on the following day, Wednesday 30th, the weather much improved and all not otherwise required were employed on chipping duties. But care was needed to maintain balance on the slippery decks and to avoid touching any bare metal with ungloved hands. By noon I was able to report to the Captain that we were once more ready for battle.

Crew of HMS *Scylla* using steam hoses to clear decks whilst on patrol in North Atlantic

Chipping away the ice and snow from HMS *Vansittart* while on convoy duty in the Arctic

CHAPTER 18

WOLFSCHANZE - WOLF'S LAIR

Wednesday, 30 December, 1942

Wolfschanze

Far distant from the Arctic in a bunker in Rastenburg, East Prussia, Hitler was holding an evening meeting with senior officers of the Wehrmacht: the Heer (the army), the Luftwaffe, and the Kriegsmarine. Strangely, he was spouting forth on how much better the Royal Navy was than his own navy. He was complaining that it was possible for the Royal Navy to sail the length of the Mediterranean Sea without challenge. His mood was not the best and, in a high pitched voice, he continued to run down his own fleet:[59]

> *...our own navy is but a copy of the British and a very poor one at that. The ships are not in operational readiness; they are lying idle in the fjords, utterly useless like so much old iron.*

Vice-Admiral Theodore Krancke was not happy, but he held his tongue. When someone at the meeting expressed the view that convoys would not sail to Murmansk at that time of the year, Krancke took the opportunity to take a piece of paper out of his briefcase, saying, " I have just received this signal from Kriegsmarine Operations Room!" Written on a piece of redcoloured paper entitled, *SECRET! OFFICERS ONLY,* with the time 13:45 stamped on it, was this message, which Krancke read out:

```
U-boat reports by short signal a convoy 50 miles
south of Bear Island, course 070°, speed 12 knots.
Convoy consists of six steamers. Weak escort.
ViceAdmiral Krancke inform Führer that C-in-C,
Navy, approves in principle the operational use of
the decision of Group North dependent on the fact
that according to the existing information the
escort with the convoy is not in fact superior.
```

This information caught Hitler's attention immediately and he enquired if German forces could reach the convoy in time to attack it? Krancke said it was possible and proceeded to inform Hitler of the distance of his own ships in Altenfjord from the convoy; the convoy's speed; and where the convoy would be when the German Navy encountered them. This news assuaged Hitler's ire.

It would take another five hours before the *Admiral Hipper* and the other battle cruiser, the *Lützow*, would be ready to sail out of Altenfjord. It would be another 16 hours before they would reach the convoy around 09:00 the next morning – Thursday, 31st December. And, importantly, they would have opportunity to attack JW51B in the half light.

Operation Rainbow (*Regenbögen*) was the plan the Kriegsmarine had to destroy the next convoy to Murmansk – and it was now apparent this was to be JW51B. The German chain of command was exasperating. Hitler in Wolfschanze would have to give his permission for Regenbögen to commence. After this, the procedure to be followed was:

1. The head of Kriegsmarine in Wolfschanze, Admiral Theodore Krancke, to convey the order to
2. Grand Admiral Erich Raeder in Berlin, who gave the order to
3. Admiral Rolf Carls, C-in-C Gruppe Nord, Kiel on the northern coast of Germany, who then passed it on to
4. Admiral Northern Waters, Otto Klüber, who was stationed in Narvik, Norway, and who then transmitted the order to
5. Vice-Admiral Oskar Kummetz on the *Hipper* in Altenfjord.

There were four U-boats positioned off Bjørnøya (Bear Island) and eight warships anchored in Altenfjord. These were *Hipper*, *Lützow*, and the six destroyers – *Richard Beitzen*, *Theodor Riedel*, *Friedrich Eckoldt*, *Z29*, *Z30*, and *Z31*. When news came of a convoy, Operation Rainbow would commence with the eight warships sailing from Altenfjord in two forces. One group would attack the Royal Navy cruisers, and the other group would attack the convoy itself.

Admiral Hipper, Norway, 1942

Hitler had given firm orders that the capital ships *Hipper* and *Lützow* should not manoeuvre themselves into danger. Also, there was another plan incorporated into Regenbögen – Operation Aurora. When Regenbögen had been completed successfully, the heavy cruiser *Lützow,* in accord with Operation Aurora, would move out into the Atlantic to attack merchant shipping. There is no doubt that Hitler's order of caution to Admiral Oskar Kummetz hindered bold action.

CHAPTER 19

THE KRIEGSMARINE IN ALTENFJORD

Prior to receiving notice from the Wolfschanze, via Berlin, and then Kiel, Admiral Klüber had anticipated that Operation Regenbögen would be implemented. He had flown from Narvik to Altenfjord and had boarded the cruiser *Köln* which was across the inlet from Kummetz.

Following the message from *U-354* at 12:42 concerning the convoy, he gave an order to Admiral Kummetz in the *Hipper*:[60]

```
Hipper and six destroyers - three hours notice.
```

There was excitement. The Germans were not accustomed to being at sea as frequently as the British sailors. Sailors of the Kriegsmarine would be at anchor for months in the fjords, cut off from the ocean. However, now there was the opportunity for action. Each rank began his work: navigators gathering their charts; engineers firing up boilers; signals being sent requesting tugs for the *Hipper* and the Lützow to assist in leaving their anchorages; minesweepers to ensure the opening to the inlet was free of mines; and the anti-torpedo nets surrounding the German vessels to be drawn aside. It was Admiral Raeder in Berlin who sent a signal to Admiral Carls:

```
In view of the U-boat's short signal Naval Staff
agrees in principle to Operation Rainbow. In
addition, examine possibility of operating Lützow
in a separate operation.
```

Carls then sent a signal to Klüber and to Kummetz in Altenfjord:[61]

Kummetz with Hipper, Lützow, and six destroyers to operate against convoy JW51B Operational Command by Admiral Klüber.

Cover name 'Rainbow'. Sail as soon as possible. Report time.

Speed of JW51B between seven and twelve Knots. Position of JW51B at midnight 31st [estimated] to be in the area between 75°30' and 71°30' north, 36° and 34° east.

It is desirable to capture single ships. There is to be no time wasted in rescuing enemy crews. It would be of value only to take a few captains and other prisoners with a view to interrogation. The rescue of enemy survivors by enemy forces is not desirable.

[This would appear to mean that rescue ships, for example, could be attacked to prevent them carrying out rescue work.]

The operation is forbidden south of 70° north.

Contact with the Luftwaffe should be maintained with Admiral Klüber.

The *Lützow* in Altenfjord

At 14:10 Kummetz sent a signal to Klüber:

> Intend to pass through the net boom at Kaafjord at 17:00. Request to be told own U-boat situation.

At 14:30 Admiral Klüber's motor launch took him and his officers from the cruiser *Köln* past the defensive nets surrounding the *Hipper* to its boarding platform. When Klüber boarded, he was afforded the customary piping aboard to which an Admiral's rank was entitled. There was to be a meeting with Admiral Kummetz, *Hipper's* commander, and Captain Stange, *Lützow's* commander. The conversations were centred on one topic – JW51B and its destruction.

Klüber spoke first saying that, according to the information he held, JW51B was heavily protected. Perhaps the two cruisers which left the Kola Inlet on 27 December were with the convoy, and he knew that there were perhaps three to four British submarines in the area. Klüber provided the information that submarines *U-354* and *U-626* were shadowing the convoy. They would have to have a few hours of daylight to make effective use of their guns. They were not to use torpedoes except in situations where they would be certain of hitting merchant ships.

Klüber reiterated Hitler's warning – that the German Navy should not put their ships at risk when encountering enemy warships. The *Hipper* and the Lützow, in particular, were advised to be especially carefully of torpedoes launched by Royal Navy destroyers. It would be difficult to spot torpedo tracks in the half light, admonished Klüber. Klüber handed over to Admiral Kummetz who detailed how he was going to deal with JW51B.

Kummetz stated that the convoy was sailing eastward. The *Kampfgruppe* (Battle Group) would sail in two groups separate from each other, with the *Lützow* 75 miles south of the *Hipper*. At 08:00 on the morning of the 31st, the two heavy cruisers would turn to the east to approach the convoy from the rear. The three destroyers accompanying each heavy cruiser would be 15 miles apart and in front of their heavy cruiser. The U-boats shadowing JW51B would provide the latest information after daybreak.

The *Hipper* would attack first from the north. This would cause the British destroyers to break away from convoy JW51B; the convoy would then have to steer south which would mean they would be running into the guns of the *Lützow*. After the completion of Operation Regenbögen the Lützow was to break away from her destroyers and sail alone to initiate Operation Aurora. Although Kummetz wanted the *Kampfgruppe* to attack the convoy with great force, at the back of his mind were Hitler's dispiriting words:[62]

```
Procedure on meeting the enemy: avoid a superior
force, otherwise destroy according to tactical
situation.
```

This order revealed a lack of trust on the Führer's part in his Kriegsmarine. No captain in charge of a heavy cruiser would ever put his vessel in danger deliberately. Therefore, Admiral Kummetz on the *Hipper* and Captain Stange on the *Lützow* had been gaslit by the Führer even before the battle began. The meeting on board the *Hipper* finished at 15:30. Klüber returned to Narvik, and Stange to the *Lützow*. The crew of the *Hipper* were busy with preparations for going to sea: doctors were making sure they had sufficient medical supplies on board; the gunnery officers were making sure that equipment was in working order; and technicians were testing the radar sets.

The *Admiral Hipper* from the air with anti-torpedo nets surrounding it

CHAPTER 20

ADMIRAL KUMMETZ'S TASK FORCE

LEAVES ALTENFJORD

Wednesday, 30 December, 1942

At 16:45 the anti-torpedo nets were opened. The captains of the six destroyers were on their respective bridges. Each sailor on board was anticipating the order to leave the anchorage. At 17:00 they still had not passed the boom. The tug which was to tow the *Hipper* out of the harbour had not appeared. Eventually it came, 15 minutes late. The *Hipper* could now move out. However, the bridge telephone rang. The engine room reported that a pump had failed. They would have to repair it before they could proceed.

At 17:45 all repairs were completed, and the *Hipper* and the other vessels could now leave Altenfjord. This fjord was 1,400 feet (427m) deep. The wind was Force 4 and blowing between 11-15 knots (13-17mph) and the weather was favourable. There was a slight swell. As soon as the battle group were out of the fjords and into the open sea, Klüber sent a signal to the U-boats reporting that Kummetz had sailed and that from noon on the 31st they were to engage with the enemy, but only when they were certain the intended targets were indeed the enemy.[63]

At 18:40, one hour after the *Hipper* had gone past the boom, Klüber, in Narvik, sent a signal. The message was decoded and given to Kummetz on the bridge. The communication did not lift his spirits: [64]

Contrary to the operational order regarding
contact against the enemy [you are] to use caution
even against enemy of equal strength because it
is undesirable for the cruisers to take any great
risks.

Back in the Wolfschanze, it was obvious Hitler was concerned that national
morale would be affected if another renowned battleship was lost, as happened
to the *Bismarck* in 1941.

Kummetz sailed with his task force north by northwest from Altenfjord and
then northeast past North Cape at 24 knots. At 02:00 on the morning of the
31st, Kummetz surmised he was at 71°01'N 24°25'E and he altered course to
confront the convoy. The *Lützow* had orders to be 75 miles and 180° from the
Hipper at 08:00. Stange had reckoned that the *Hipper* would be at 73°40'N 28°E
at that time in the morning.[65]

Convoy and Kriegsmarine locations at 02:00, 31 December, 1942

At 05:00 the *Hipper* picked up a radio signal from *U-354* to Narvik which read:[66]

> From 20.30 forced under water, bombed. Last location escort Qu. 4513 AC [Course] around 120° 13 knots, weather conditions very good, advancing...

Kummetz was not altogether sure the information was correct, but if he did not alter the *Hipper's* course and that of the three accompanying destroyers, he would not encounter the convoy.

Therefore, he instructed the destroyers to change course 20 miles to the south. Kummetz gave another order also. He asked his task force from 06:00 onward, when the visibility fell to below 6 miles, to operate radar for two minutes every ten minutes lest they run into the convoy unawares.

At 05:45 Captain Stange on the *Lützow* received a communication from Admiral Klüber in Narvik which contained details of an additional operation he had not anticipated, and may further explain his hesitant behaviour in the Battle of the Barents Sea:[67]

> FT 01:53 from North Sea Commander SSD to B.d.K and Lützow:
>
> After completion Regenbögen, intending to release Lützow within the North Sea northwards 70 degrees north between 5 degrees east and 35 degrees east.
>
> Mission: cruiser-war, detect enemy shipping traffic, attack single cruisers and poorly secured escorts. Cue for release Aurora . . .
>
> Development of Regenbögen is crucial for release . . . Proceed only if Lützow has at least half of artillery and torpedo ammunition left.
>
> Break off Lützow's being at sea independently as soon as enemy units can be recognised from heavy cruiser upwards or after collection of enemy forces becomes probable following considerable success . . . Further information later.

Stange wrote in his diary:[68]

The receipt of this FT creates a new situation for me in so far as contrary to the original plans...it is now no longer possible to talk the operation through with B.d.K [Befehlshaber der Kreuzer–Admiral Commanding Cruisers] in detail, neither can I request documents about the enemy from him...

At 07:18 the *Hipper* saw two shadows on the radar. The destroyer *Friedrich Eckholdt* was sent to ascertain who they were. At 07:47 a larger shadow was seen and the *Hipper* turned towards it. This could be one of the tankers which was separated from the rear of the convoy. The Germans were not sure whether it was a cruiser or a merchant ship they were seeing. Whilst they were deliberating another six shadows appeared on the screen and the captains and officers were now certain that they had caught up with Convoy JW51B.

At 08:00 on 31st December the *Lützow* was where she was ordered to be. Captain Stange thought the convoy was 80 miles to the north, and about to be caught between the two claws of one lobster. The plan which Vice-Admiral Kummetz had devised was working. At 07:58, he had sent a message to his task force:

```
Alarm - Square 4395.
```

Everything was now in place for the Battle of the Barents Sea to commence.

CHAPTER 21

U-354 STALKS JW51B

Wednesday, 30 December, 1942

On the morning of 30 December, Kapitänleutnant Karl-Heinz Herschleb was tracking JW51B in *U-354*. In Narvik, a little after midday Otto Klüber, Admiral in charge of Northern Waters, received a message from Herschleb informing him that the convoy was on course 100°. He reported between six and ten merchant vessels with a number of destroyers and one light cruiser.

U-354 kept ahead of the convoy, moving slowly to the south of it. The submarine descended to periscope depth to observe the lead ships. The periscope was lowered, and three torpedoes were fired. In the U-boat, Herschleb and his crew were counting on a stopwatch the seconds it would take for the three black fish to reach their targets. No one heard the noise of an explosion. He put up the periscope. Herschleb was disappointed. At the last moment the convoy zigzagged and the torpedoes glided past the stern of the ships.[69]

He would not have another opportunity to release further torpedoes at this stage. In the evening nightfall he surfaced and sent another signal to Dönitz in Germany and Klüber in Norway:[70]

```
Convoy in square AC 4189. The convoy split up.
Zigzag of up to 80°. About 10 steamers, several
destroyers and one cruiser. Fired three torpedoes
but these missed because of zigzag. Weather good
apart from snow squalls.
```

He began to pursue the convoy again, this time on the surface. In the darkness Herschleb was listening to the reverberations of the convoy through hydrophones which were picking up echoes from their propellers. He continued to do this until 20:15 when he heard another sound – a Royal Navy destroyer closing fast. *U-354* submerged immediately.

The destroyer was HMS *Obdurate*. She was south of the convoy and had picked up an echo from *U-354*. The ASDIC operator had given the bridge coordinates to allow them to pursue *U-354*. Captain Sclater on *Obdurate* was at first going to ram the U-boat. But, before he could do so, the submarine submerged into the cold waters of the Arctic.

Sclater notified Commander Sherbrooke in the *Onslow*, who was on the far side of the convoy and too distant to help; however, Sherbrooke sent a message to *Obedient* to assist *Obdurate*. Both *Obdurate* and *Obedient* tried to ping the hull of the *U-boat* with sonar to receive an echo. The echo would provide the exact location of *U-354*. After a short while, they obtained an echo 1,000 yards ahead of them. Depth-charges were thrown from the *Obedient*. However, after the explosions there was no debris or oil spillage to see. They lost contact with *U-354* although they continued for two hours to try to locate it. According to Royal Navy rules, a *Uboat* search should not continue beyond two hours to ensure that overmuch fuel is not consumed. The two destroyers returned to the convoy.

Captain Kinloch on HMS *Obedient* was not certain that they had located a submarine and in a communication to Commander Sherbrooke at 23:14 that night, said:

```
Four  depth-charges  dropped  on  non-submarine
contact.
```

At 23:56, when he was certain that there were no propeller noises, Herschleb took *U-354* to the surface and sent a message to Admiral Klüber:[71]

```
From 20.30 depth-charged and forced to submerge.
Last position of convoy was AC 6451 and mean
course about 120°, speed thirteen knots. Weather
very good and I am pursuing. [The correct course
of the convoy was 90° and the speed was 9 knots
(10mph)]
```

The convoy was 200 miles from Altenfjord, the chief port for the northern fleet of the Kriegsmarine. The Admiralty sent a signal to Sherbrooke that there was a lot of chatter on German radio. Perhaps this indicated that the convoy had been spotted. The truth was that the Germans were preparing for a major surface attack because of Herschleb's intelligence about the convoy.

Hitler was of the opinion that there would be an allied assault at some point on the Norwegian coast and that his heavy battleships should be protected to make sure they would be available if the invasion happen in the north. Therefore, the substance of the messages which would come to Admiral Kummetz from Berlin was:

1. Use the warships with caution.

2. Forbid the warships from going too close to British warships, unless there is certainty that they will win and that there will be no German losses.

Admiral Kummetz felt Hitler had placed a yoke around his neck, hindering him from waging war effectively. Later on the night of the 30th, Hitler heard that the Kriegsmarine vessels had sailed and that there was a possibility they would encounter the convoy on the morning of 31st December.

Three U-boats in submarine pen at Trondheim, Norway

German U-boats outside submarine pen in Trondheim, Norway

CHAPTER 22

BATTLE OF THE BARENTS SEA

A FOREBODING

Thursday, 31 December, 1942 – 04:00

HMS *Achates* was constantly zig-zagging on the port side of the convoy. At 04:00 Lieutenant Peyton Jones reached the bridge to begin the morning watch. There would be another four hours before he would get some sleep again. The night sky was cloudless and the sea state was Force 4 on the Beaufort scale (12-16 knots). It was very dark and deadly cold. Peyton Jones was reflecting that it was the seventh day since they had left Iceland and in two more days they would reach Murmansk. He and the crew were weary through resisting the attacks they had experienced during the voyage.

The German Battle group was approximately 200 miles from the convoy on December 31 at 02:00

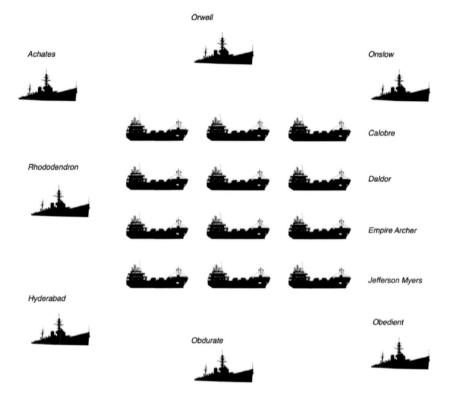

Convoy JW51B on the morning of 31 December 1942. Three merchant vessels were missing – *Dover Hill*, because she had suffered storm damage five days after leaving Loch Ewe and had returned; *Chester Valley*, and *John Latrobe* had strayed from the convoy and had not yet been located.

At 08:00 Sub-lieutenant Anthony Davidson came to the bridge to relieve Peyton Jones. Davidson would cover the forenoon watch from 08:00-12:00. Day was breaking and darkness was lifting to a degree. Peyton Jones informed Davidson that the minesweeper HMS *Bramble*, the trawler *Vizalma*, and two merchant vessels were still separated from the convoy. Davidson glimpsed the form of two vessels on the horizon and both agreed that they were, most likely, two of the boats which were still unlocated. Captain AT Johns arrived, but the ships were now out of sight. Peyton Jones went below to warm himself and get a bite to eat.[72]

Captain Sherbrooke, First Lieutenant Lewis King, and navigator Peter Wyatt were on the bridge of the Onslow. It was 07:40 and the morning watch would end in twenty minutes. The crew on watch would be relieved and go down below for breakfast and a little sleep. Sherbrooke said quietly to Lewis King:

Number One, I have a feeling something is going to happen today, and I want you to see that all the hands are breakfasted by 09:00 and changed into clean underwear.

King delivered Sherbrooke's order and then filled in the deck log – just as in a diary:

HMS Onslow Thursday 31st December, 1942

From Iceland to Murmansk and at sea
Five on sick list
Propellers: 111rpm
Mean course: 090° (due east)
Wind: NW (on port quarter), Force 2
Sea: Smooth with long low swell
Barometer: 1004 millibars
Sea Temperature: 41° Farenheit
Air Temperature: 25° Farenheit

At 08:00, every sailor was satisfied. Those who were coming off watch were looking forward to food and sleep, and those who were going on watch had been fed and were warm and had four hours sleep.

At 08:20, the watchkeeper on the port side of the *Hyderabad*, saw two destroyers on a course of 180° (sailing to the south). The *Hyderabad* thought that they were the Russian vessels the convoy was expecting. Therefore, they did not inform Sherbrooke on the *Onslow*. A few minutes after this though, a watchkeeper on the *Obdurate* which was zig-zagging south of the convoy, reported that he saw two destroyers sailing south by south west on a course of 210°. Captain Sclater on the *Obdurate* reported this to Sherbrooke. The message was sent at 08:30, but because the communication had to be signal lamped via the *Obedient*, it was 08:45 before the *Onslow* received it. When Sherbrooke and Peter Wyatt saw the message – *Bearing 210° two destroyers* – they reached for their binoculars and scanned the ocean to the south. They did not see anything. The *Obdurate* turned to port and made for the rear of the convoy.

At the rear of the convoy, Sclater observed three destroyers which he did not recognise. They were sailing north in line. At 09:15, Sclater noted that the unrecognised destroyers had turned to the west and away from the *Obdurate*, but then altered to the north-west again. He was still not certain who they were. Sclater asked for a message to be signalled to them via the Aldis lamp. They did not answer. Then, he saw an amber flash from one of them. The vessel had fired on them. It was 09:30 and the German destroyers were 4.5 miles away. The shells fell a distance away from the *Obdurate*. Sclater sent a message to Sherbrooke in the *Onslow* that the enemy had arrived.

On the *Onslow* Sherbrooke was observing a merchant vessel which had fallen behind the convoy. He saw flickers of flame on the horizon. Enemy vessels were firing at the tanker. He announced 'Action Stations'. The torpedo tubes on the *Onslow* were made ready for firing.

On the *Achates,* Captain Johns had received the order to go to 'Action Stations'. 'Muzzle flashes to the rear of the convoy,' explained Johns when Peyton Jones reached the bridge. The Captain indicated they were going to put into action the plan agreed eight days ago at Loch Ewe. Sherbrooke had said on that day:

> *Because there is darkness for long periods at this time of the year, naval attacks will be more likely than air attacks. Therefore, if the Kriegsmarine appears, Onslow, Obedient, Oribi, Orwell, and Obdurate will move from being on both sides of the convoy to the side where the Germans present themselves.*
> *Achates and Bulldog will lay down smoke in the attack and they must position themselves between the enemy and the convoy. Under cover of the smoke, the convoy will turn away under the command of Commodore Melhuish. [Bulldog was no longer with the convoy as it had returned to port because of storm damage.]*

The role of the destroyers was to put themselves between the enemy and the merchant ships in accordance with the plan. Lieutenant Peyton Jones left the bridge to check that each sailor was closed up in his station between the decks.

After Peyton Jones had left the bridge, Captain Johns pressed the button in the middle of the brass plate which had the words: 'MAKE SMOKE'. Down below, the engineers heard a loud bell and opened the 'fuel injection valves' so that more oil than could be burned was forced into the furnaces. Impenetrable black smoke rose up into the air and a long lock of curls swirled past the stern of the *Achates* and out over the surface of the ocean. A protective shield was being laid down and the convoy was now disappearing from the *Admiral Hipper's* sight. The two corvettes *Hyderabad* and *Rhododendron* arrived to support the *Achates*. The merchant vessels at the rear of the convoy deployed smoke floats also.

The convoy altered course to the south. However, the *Achates*– which was to the southwest of the German heavy cruiser – was silhouetted against the grey sky and it was obvious she was the vessel laying down the smoke screen. She was now a clear target.

A Royal Navy destroyer laying down smoke

The 14 merchant ships in JW51B, under the command of Commodore RA Melhuish, which made it safely to Murmansk, apart from the Ballot, which foundered at the entrance to Kola Inlet:

EMPIRE ARCHER
Commodore of convoy, Captain Melhuish's ship.
British. 141 vehicles, 18 tanks, 21 fighters, 4,376 tons general cargo.

DALDORCH
British. 264 vehicles, 1,744 tons general cargo.

EMPIRE EMERALD
British. 5,500 tons oil fuel, 5,280 tons aviation fuel.

PONTFIELD
British. Tanker Grounded at Kola Inlet but towed to Rosta drydock for repairs.

CHESTER VALLEY
US. 2 vehicles, 25 tanks, 10 fighters, 4 bombers, 250 tons fuel, 4,371 tons general cargo.

PUERTO RICAN
US. 14 vehicles, 23 tanks, 15 fighters, 8 bombers, 100 tons fuel, 5,345 general cargo.

EXECUTIVE VALLEY
US. 139 vehicles, 4 bombers, 450 tons fuel, 450 tons fuel, 5,.534 tons general cargo.

R.W. EMERSON
US. 160 vehicles, 25 tanks, 18 fighters, 0 tons fuel, 5,534 tons general cargo.

JEFFERSON MEYERS
US. 376 vehicles, 4 bombers, 500 tons fuel, 5,336 tons general cargo

VERMONT
US. 299 vehicles, 4 bombers, 300 tons fuel, 4,048 tons general cargo.

YORKMAR
US. 188 vehicles, 150 tons fuel, 5,326 tons general cargo.

JOHN H. LaTROBE
US. 191 vehicles, 58 tanks, 10 fighters, 4 bombers, 640 tons fuel, 4,397 tons general cargo.

CALOBRE
Panamanian. 166 vehicles, 8 tanks, 250 tons fuel, 4,534 tons general cargo.

BALLOT
Panamanian. General Cargo. Went aground and abandoned at entrance to Kola Inlet. Some cargo recovered by Russian barges.

CHAPTER 23

THE BATTLE OF THE BARENTS SEA

THE *KRIEGSMARINE* ENCROACHES

Thursday, 31 December 1942 – 08:00

At 08:00, Rudolf Stange, captain of the battlecruiser *Lützow*, estimated Convoy JW51B was around 80 miles to his north. He was in position to accomplish Admiral Kummetz's plan to pinch JW51B from both sides. Kummetz, to the north of the *Lützow*, had sighted the convoy and at 07.58 sent a signal to his *Kampfgruppe* (battle group):[73]

```
Alarm Square 4395.
```

He also sent a signal to the destroyer *Eckholdt* that she should continue observing the convoy.

At 08:02, Kummetz sent another message to the whole *Kampfgruppe*:

```
Hipper attacks from north at first light.
```

To be in the best position to attack the convoy at first light, Kummetz sailed east at 20 knots. He wrote at this time:[74]

I decide, in order to make use of the coming twilight hours which are essential for this operation, to attack with Hipper at dawn even if the destroyers are not in company. Eckholdt must for the time being remain as convoy shadower… the destroyers are not to join up with the Hipper and Lützow while it is still dark because of the danger of getting mixed up.

At 08:30, the *Obdurate* spotted the *Eckholdt* and the other German vessels which were in company at the rear of the convoy. Sherbrooke, the Royal Navy escort commander, ordered the *Obdurate* to go to the rear of the convoy to investigate.

At 09:07, when morning light was breaking through, Kummetz organised his six destroyers. The signaller in the *Hipper* began to send out messages ordering ships to gather with their respective cruisers:

```
Beitzen group [Beitzen, Eckholdt, and Z29] to
Hipper and Z31 group [Z31, Theodore Riedel, and
Z30] to Lützow.
```

The German operators were still sending the signal when look-outs on the *Hipper* reported the outline of ships, and estimated there were possibly five at least. Five minutes after this at 09:15, Kummetz wrote:

Visibility very poor. Everything seems hazy. Cannot make out whether I am dealing with friend or foe. A total of ten ships now in sight, some of which look like destroyers. It cannot be said for certain whether our own shadowing destroyers are not among them. It is therefore essential to exchange recognition signals.[74]

The term fog of war is used to describe how confused warfare can seem when immersed in it; such was Kummetz's situation. He asked for a recognition signal to be transmitted to the nearest destroyer. He did not receive a reply. However, a separate incoming message from the *Eckholdt* that Z-39 and *Beitzen* were 'formed up round the convoy' arrived. Next, came a message from Captain Stange. He was miles away to the south on the *Lützow*. He was closing on the convoy at 26 knots and on a north-easterly course. Gun flares were seen on the horizon. Kummetz thought that they came from German ships. He was correct. The *Eckholdt*, Z-29, and *Beitzen* were firing at the *Obdurate*. The *Hipper* was closing on the convoy from the northwest. She had 8" guns, full of high explosive – the kind which would do maximum damage to the steel plates of the convoy vessels.

Thursday, 31 December, 1942 – 09:40

In the half-light, Hartmann, the *Hipper's* captain, observed through his binoculars the dark contours of the merchant vessels eight miles away on his starboard bow. They were fully laden with arms for Russia. He also saw a British destroyer laying down a screen of dense, black smoke the length of the convoy. The *Achates* was pulling a huge black theatre curtain across the scene. Soon the convoy would be safe and out of sight. The curtain of smoke debarred the *Hipper* from penetrating; on the other side was the unknown. Destroyers could be waiting, ready to launch a torpedo attack. Hartmann asked permission of Admiral Kummetz to fire on the *Achates*. He received permission. He turned the *Hipper* to port to enable the four turrets with two guns per turret to aim at the British destroyer. When the *Hipper's* eight guns fired a salvo (each shell weighing 250lbs (113.4kg)), close to a ton of explosives would hurtle to the target at 1,000mph. The shells would take about 23 seconds to span the eight miles between the *Hipper* and the *Achates*.

Hipper's guns fired at 09:42. A broadside of eight shells fell close to the British destroyer. Within 12 seconds (each gun could fire five shells per minute) the *Hipper* fired again. This time the shells straddled the *Achates* with perhaps one landing on the ship.

The *Hipper* firing.

Lieutenant Loftus Peyton Jones explained what happened when the *Hipper* commenced firing:[75]

Having ascertained that all was ready below – ammunition supply parties, the TS crew, the fire and repair parties and first aid crews, I climbed up to Y gundeck on top of the after superstructure, but it was very hard to see what was going on.

It was about 09:40, and though the southern sky was slowly lightening, to the north the black snow clouds merged into the sea, leaving no horizon.

Then, suddenly, out of the blackness appeared more gunflashes, the first that I had seen, and great fountains of water thrown up about a cable's length away. Big shells these, which exploded on impact.

After the first salvo, Captain Johns increased speed and at the same time he turned the vessel suddenly and sharply, putting the ship on her side. The *Achates'* guns returned fire. At eight miles distance, the destroyer's guns were at the edge of their range. Her four 4" guns could only fire a salvo of 124lbs, in comparison to the 2,000lbs from the 8" guns of the Hipper. Peyton Jones recorded:[76]

The next salvo arrived, much closer this time with eight huge splashes, some on either side of the ship. The enemy had found the range and we had been straddled. Despite our now zig-zagging course the next two salvos were equally accurate and a particular near-miss abreast the bridge on the port side sent showers of splinters scything across the deck and drenched the guns' crews in icy spray. Then as Onslow, with Orwell in close company, closed the distance, our adversary, which turned out to be the 8-inch cruiser Hipper, altered course away northwards under threat of torpedo attack from the destroyers, and we were left to assess the damage.

Peyton Jones carried out a damage assessment and discovered that it was worse than he had first anticipated. Many of the shrapnel shards from the *Hipper's* shelling had penetrated the side of the boat and had wreaked havoc between decks. The port bow of the *Achates* was perforated like a colander and the gashes were letting the seawater gush in. Electric cables were ripped. Sailors' cupboards were distorted, and the contents scattered haphazardly across their quarters. The tables in the mess were floating awkwardly in the flood that was pouring in through the ship's wounded side. Peyton Jones further describes the carnage he encountered during his damage assessment:[77]

In the dim light it was difficult not to trip over the bodies of the killed or wounded which lay in passage ways and messdecks. I was much relieved when the Chief, Peter Wright, rigged up some emergency lighting and the Doctor, James MacFarlane, appeared to take charge of the casualties. Calm and unruffled amidst the chaos, he organised their removal to the first aid post, quieting the more seriously injured with shots of morphia.

I went up to the bridge to make a quick report to the Captain before returning to help Peter Wright organise the repair parties. I found that we were continuing to lay smoke across the stern of the convoy which was now making an emergency turn to starboard to steer south-east. Fortunately the wind was north-westerly so that the lines of smoke blew down along the convoy's track.

After speaking to the Captain, Peyton Jones returned to the mess deck in the forepart of the ship. The repair crew were doing their best to dam the holes. The ocean poured in with each zig-zag to port. Worse still, the holes below the waterline were like streams in spate, with a constant rush of incoming water. Because the vessel was insulated for the Arctic, the sailors had to rip this away from the ship's plates before they could attempt a repair. This used up valuable time. When they had pulled the insulation away, they saw that the holes were sharp and ragged – the majority were between half an inch and six inches in diameter. Some were larger and not easy to stem.

The 8" guns on the *Admiral Hipper*

It is reckoned that this is the battle cruiser *The Admiral Hipper* firing at HMS *Glowworm* and sinking her on 8 April, 1940. *The Glowworm* is laying down smoke.

On the stokers' mess deck, one deck below, matters were worse. The inflow of water was greater and it appeared that one of the plates in the hull had split. There was a deep pool in this area and the seawater was pouring down to the deck below where the armoury and the shell room was. Neither the pumps nor any of the other equipment was of use. The only solution was to close the watertight doors throughout the mess deck and to strengthen the bulkheads. Within a few minutes, these three large areas – the armoury, the shell room, and the stokers' mess rooms – were inundated. Because of this, the bow of the boat went below the waterline. The flooding in other parts of the ship was controlled to a degree and there was some hope the situation could be retrieved. Although they were still laying down smoke to protect the convoy, the ship's speed was greatly reduced to prevent the hull splitting.

CHAPTER 24

ONSLOW AND ORWELL

APPROACH THE *HIPPER*

Thursday, 31 December, 1942 – 09:44

It was now 09:44, and the two destroyers, *Onslow* and *Orwell*, were moving at speed towards the *Hipper*. Lookouts on the *Hipper* saw the *Onslow* approaching to the south of her bow. Admiral Kummetz knew immediately that the *Onslow* was in a perfect position to release a torpedo. Captain Sherbrooke understood that the threat of releasing a torpedo was more powerful than the act of doing so. If he had torpedoes, the *Hipper* would be wary of him. The *Onslow* veered to port when she closed, and the *Hipper* thought she had released a torpedo. But she had not. She was also turning to keep herself between the convoy and the *Hipper*. The captain of the *Hipper* wrote in his log:[78]

> *09:44: A destroyer approached from the south-east and then put her helm hard-over. She had fired torpedoes.*

Harmann ordered that the stern of the ship should be turned towards the *Onslow* and the *Orwell*. This was the standard action if you thought torpedoes were coming your way. Any captain would want to present the smallest target to the enemy.

Sherbrooke's plan was working. In trying to protect herself, the *Hipper* had turned away from the convoy. Although Admiral Kummetz, in the flagship of the task force, had been made to turn away from the convoy, he had great admiration for Sherbrooke's handling of matters. He wrote in his log:[79]

The [British] destroyers conducted themselves very skilfully. They placed themselves in such a position between Hipper and the convoy that it was impossible to get near the ships. They also made very effective use of a smoke-screen with which they tried to hide the merchant ships. They tried to dodge Hipper's fire by taking avoiding action and using smoke. Their relative position forced Hipper to run the risk of a torpedo attack while trying to use her guns on the ships.

Time: 09:45-09:55

At 09:45, as the two destroyers *Onslow* and *Orwell* engaged the *Hipper*, the convoy altered course from east to southeast at a speed of 9 knots. Sherbrooke was a little concerned about the German destroyers. There was no sign of them and he judged that they were going to attack the merchant vessels. Because of this, he chose to return to the convoy with *Obedient*, *Obdurate*, and *Orwell*. However, Sherbrooke was unaware that Kummetz had asked the German destroyers to stay with him in the engagement with the *Onslow* and the *Orwell*. The convoy was not in any danger from these German destroyers.[80]

Time: 09:57-10:04

Admiral Kummetz recognised that Sherbrooke had tricked him in that first attack. He altered *Hipper's* course to the east at 09:57 for a second attack. Kummetz wanted to fire a broadside at *Onslow* and *Orwell* with his eight big guns. However, the two cruisers preempted his strategy and by strong shelling caused Hitler's heavy battle cruiser to turn away into the darkness of the north-east. The *Hipper* was driven away from the convoy once again. (Hitler's orders must have been ringing in the Admiral's head – the major battleships should not put themselves in danger from enemy forces). Although this was favourable for the convoy in one way, in another way they were turning south and into the other claw of the lobster, the *Lützow*, which was steaming from the south-west to the north-east.

At 10:04, the *Hipper* attempted her third attack. Kummetz chose to sail to the south-east and run directly at *Onslow* and *Orwell*. He kept on this course for four minutes firing at the two British destroyers with his 8" guns. The two Royal Navy vessels kept stubbornly on their westward course, zig-zagging to avoid the shells. Again, they were cutting *Hipper* off from accessing the convoy.[81]

Time: 10:08-10:20

At 10:08, Kummetz ceased firing and turned the *Hipper* towards the north-east again. Perhaps he wanted to draw breath. At 10:13, he began his fourth attack. Kummetz was going to fire another broadside. At the same time, he sent a signal to his own task force:

```
Hipper to north of convoy and there are four enemy
destroyers between us and the convoy.
```

The signal was incorrect because *Onslow* and *Orwell* were the only boats attacking the *Hipper*. *Obedient* and *Obdurate* had sailed south towards the convoy. The *Hipper* increased speed and at the same time started firing incessantly at *Onslow* and *Orwell*. It was not a fair contest. The firepower of the *Hipper's* guns was ten times more powerful than the Royal Navy destroyers' guns. Kummetz also knew that the steel plates protecting his ship were thick enough to stop the shells of the British destroyers. There was going to be only one outcome to this battle.

It was possible for the lookouts on *Onslow* and *Orwell* to see the red flashes of the *Hipper's* guns. The first salvo or two went past. At 10:14 a salvo arrived which dropped closer to the *Onslow*. The next two salvos exploded 150 yards beyond the ship, and the next two on each side of the stern of the boat. The *Hipper* now had the *Onslow's* range.

At 10:18, the radar operator on the *Onslow* saw the shells coming towards him on his screen as he was relaying information to the bridge:

```
Salvo coming...coming towards...coming towards...
```

The poor lad had only a blink of time to understand that the shells in the incoming salvo were going to fall on him before he died. There was a terrifying explosion behind the bridge. One shell split the funnel for the boiler room. It tore it from top to bottom, and live steam was spouting into the air under high pressure. The screaming of the steam was terrifying.

The razor-sharp pieces of shrapnel killed a boy from Scotland who had been on watch to the rear of the bridge. Another sailor received a fatal wound, and his screaming was sending shivers through the other sailors around him. The iron shell-casing fragments had rained down on the bridge like hailstones, hitting Captain Sherbrooke. His cheek, his nose, and the left-hand side of his brow had been marred. His eye had fallen down his cheek. Sherbrooke continued to issue orders, determined that he would remain on the bridge.

In his book *73 ° North*, Dudley Pope reveals the conversation which was taking place on the bridge at that time:[82]

> *Most of A and B guns' crews killed, I'm afraid, sir.*
> *Hipper's shifted fire to Orwell.*
> *Get a report from the engine-room on this damage.*
> *You need help, sir, I've sent for the SBA [Sick Berth Attendant]*
> *No, no, I can see, said Sherbrooke. 'Where is Obedient?*
> *About five miles to the south, sir. Orwell is joining us.*
> *Yes, he'll be no good on his own.*

Before anyone could help Sherbrooke there were two large explosions like the shining of lightning at the bow of the boat. Two 8" shells from the *Hipper* had fallen on the foredeck. Immediately following, flames rose up in front of the bridge: the cordite charges for the guns had ignited, adding to the dreadful inferno. Sherbrooke knew that the next strike from the *Hipper* could obliterate the ship and its crew. He must veer away at once and reduce the speed of the ship in order to smother the major fires on board. He shouted:

> *Come hard to starboard, Pilot, make smoke and come down to fifteen knots.*

Lieutenant Marchant pushed the button 'MAKE SMOKE' and another officer shouted down the voice pipe:

> *Starboard 20, revolutions for fifteen knots!*

This swift turn deceived the *Hipper's* gunners and the next three salvos fell 30 yards past the *Onslow*. Captain Sherbrooke was informed that his ship was out of danger now, despite the fires and the damage below. Having heard this, he asked Captain Kinloch in the *Obedient* to take charge of the 17th Destroyer Flotilla. The *Onslow* was without radar, ASDIC, and front guns.

This was the conversation on the bridge when Sherbrooke agreed to go down below:[83]

> *Torps (Capt. Marchant), you take over here while I go below and get patched*
> *up. Tell Obedient what's happened and order him to take over temporary*
> *command. Do what you can with the fires, and as we aren't much use now it*
> *would be a good idea to fall back on the convoy and home the cruisers. Keep*
> *me informed.*

Sherbrooke, who was now almost blind, had to be assisted down the ladder to his cabin. The little cabin was on the deck below the bridge. There was a bunk, a desk, and a sink. The electric light was not working due to the damage, but there was a storm lantern. Sherbrooke was put into his bed and his face was patched up as much as it possibly could be. Not one word of complaint emanated from Sherbrooke and when they had finished the repair work to his face, they gave him a shot of morphia. (For the work which he performed commanding the close escort force and for remaining at his post, despite his horrific face wounds, he was awarded the Victoria Cross.)

Kummetz in the *Hipper* thought that the *Onslow* had been rendered useless and he now fixed his attention on *Orwell*. On *Orwell*, Captain Austen had seen the salvos dropping close to the *Onslow*. He was certain she was going to explode. From stem to stern she was covered in steam and smoke.

At the same time, Austen saw the *Hipper* turning to fix her attention on his ship. He pressed the 'MAKE SMOKE' button. He pondered whether he should attack the *Hipper* and fire torpedoes, or provide protection for the *Onslow*. Whilst he was pondering, he saw the *Hipper* turn away and sail into a snow squall. Her guns had ceased firing. Miraculously, *Onslow* and *Obedient* had been saved.

The splinters from the *Hipper's* shell which hit the *Onslow's* funnel gave
Captain Sherbrooke on the bridge his severe wounds.

CHAPTER 25

THE *KRIEGSMARINE*

LOSES AN OPPORTUNITY

Thursday, 31 December, 1942

Time: 10:35

Because of the wound received by Captain Robert St Vincent Sherbrooke, Captain Kinloch in the *Obedient* was now in command of the 17th Destroyer Flotilla and Convoy JW51B. He did not have full information about the situation of each boat when he took charge at 10:35. The convoy was sailing on a course of 180° (directly south). He and *Obdurate* were three miles north of the convoy and closing. HMS *Onslow*, broken and maimed, was making its way to the head of the convoy as ordered. The *Onslow* passed the *Obedient*, and when the crew of HMS *Obedient* saw the pitiable condition of the *Onslow*, they cheered and encouraged her crew on account of their great efforts. The *Onslow* had been like a small seal confronted by a killer whale and, yet, had survived.

The *Hipper* had sailed to the east at 31 knots and Captain Kinloch had no inkling as to where she might be now. There was presently a major snowsquall, and snowflakes were dancing and reeling in the air like demons, hiding boats from one another.

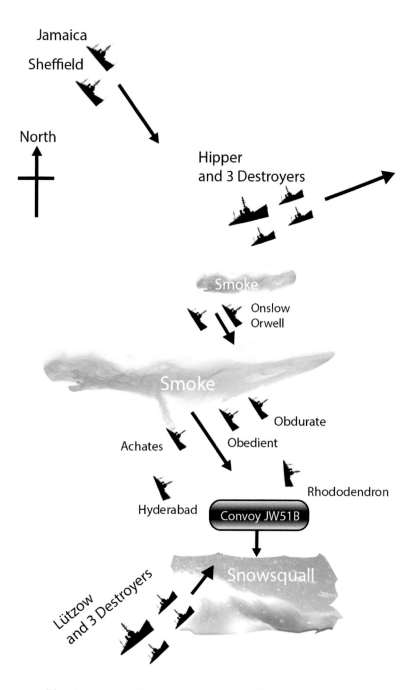

The situation at 10:30 on the morning of 31 December, 1942

Messages were coming to Kinloch from the *Rhododendron*, which was on the port side of the convoy. She intimated that she saw smoke and a large ship steaming towards JW51B; the ship was only two miles from her. The same information came from Lieutenant Commander Marchant who was on the *Onslow*. The large ship was the *Lützow*, and in company with her was her squadron. In an interview after the war, Marchant described the situation:[84]

> *At a range of about 6000 yards [5486m], on a bearing of green 40 [off the destroyer's starboard bow], silently slid into view the huge silhouette of the German pocket battleship Lützow. She was steering NNE. If, in our predicament, we could see her, surely she could see us and the...ships with us. So we simply stopped breathing and waited for the first broadside. But nothing happened! As quietly as she came into view she slid out – a ghost ship if ever there was. Many prayers winged aloft during those charged and tense minutes.*

The *Rhododendron* was in the same predicament. If the *Lützow* had seen her or fired upon her, her war and her crew's war would have been over. According to reports, Captain Sayers in the *Rhododendron* had wanted to fire on the *Lützow*. The First Lieutenant was not sure that he had heard the captain's order correctly. When he realised that he had indeed heard him correctly, he put a quiet word in his ear saying that he thought that it might not go too well with the *Rhododendron* at this point in time, if he confronted the *Lützow*. Fortunately, Sayers did not fire at the *Lützow* as she ghosted past the *Onslow*.

At 10:45 the *Lützow's* radar picked up a number of targets within the snowsquall, but the lookouts could not see anything through their binoculars. Captain Stange was perplexed. He was almost certain that inside the snowsquall were enemy vessels. Stange moved his squadron to a better position to determine the identity of the vessels he saw on the radar screen. If they turned out to be merchant ships, he would fire upon them. Stange wrote in *Lützow's* log:[85]

> *To avoid observation from Lützow being obscured by the snow squalls and smoke drifting south, I decided to proceed at low speed in the vicinity of the convoy, clear of the snow squalls, to take advantage of opportunities for attack as visibility improved.*

Stange had three destroyers with him, each with a torpedo. Two of the destroyers had five 5" guns apiece. The *Lützow* herself had six 11" guns, eight 5.9" guns, six 4.1" guns, and eight torpedoes. Stange permitted his force to approach as closely as two to three miles to the convoy without firing a shell at them. Operation Regenbögen had been devised for this very scenario, but Stange did not take the opportunity when it presented itself.

Stange continued to the north-east attempting to overtake the snowsquall. When he had done so, he returned to the south-east at 15 knots keeping to the edge of the snowsquall. If the weather cleared he would be able to identify the vessels on the radar screen. However, many are of the opinion that what was at the back of Stange's mind was the order he had received earlier from High Command that the *Lützow* was to move out into the Atlantic after Operation Regensbogen, but only if he had preserved half of his gun ammunitions and torpedoes.

Time: 11:00

About 11:00 *Lützow* was steaming south-east by east at 12 knots. The heavy cruiser was sighted by *Obedient* which was with *Obdurate* and *Orwell*. These three destroyers were moving at speed to the east of the convoy to keep themselves between the convoy and the *Lützow*.[86]

CHAPTER 26

A DESTROYER DESTROYED

Thursday 31 December, 1942

Time: 11:15

The British destroyers were doing their best to track the course of the German warships in order to position themselves between the *Lützow* and the convoy. Captain Kinloch asked the *Achates* to accompany him:

```
Join me. Prolong the line to port.
```

The *Achates* replied:

```
Holed forward. Maximum speed 15 knots.
```

The *Achates* could not go any faster because of the amount of water entering the shrapnel holes; below deck, there were now tons of water swilling around. After Kinloch understood this, he sent a signal:

```
Proceed to the head of the convoy and take Onslow
under your orders.
```

Captain Johns carried out his orders and moved out of the smoke screen he was creating. Immediately, the *Hipper* spotted the *Achates*. The German warship was heading towards the convoy from the north-east to attempt another attack.

The salvos started and, as before, the German gunners had the *Achates'* range. Captain Johns increased the *Achates'* speed, zig-zagging to avoid the shells. Lieutenant Peyton Jones was below keeping an eye on the repair work being carried out to the bow. He felt the ship's increase in speed and Captain

Johns' weaving turns. This is the reason the First Lieutenant returned to the Transmitting Station (TS) below the bridge. There, everything was composed and under control. Range and bearings for the target were coming to and going from the controlling director on the bridge who then relayed this information to the gun crews on the ship. Peyton Jones had just taken in all that was going on in the TS when he heard and experienced a huge explosion. A great shudder went through the ship. It was clear that the *Achates* had suffered a serious strike.

HMS *Achates* with the radar cabin arrowed

There were three radar operators in the 'caboose' (as they called their radar cabin above the bridge): Fred Bean from London, Ivor Roe from Manchester, and David Macdonald from Waternish in the Isle of Skye. Fred Bean wrote down his recollections for his family:[87]

The 1st three shells missed but the fourth exploded just on our port side and that is when I caught my packet. I was operator on the RDF. I was passing to the bridge ranges and bearings of Jerry, then out went all the lights. There was a terrific splash. I felt something go into my right shoulder and hand. There was also another RDF rating with me [David Macdonald], and he had his stomach grazed and also Ivor the Wireless Mike, a piece caught his ear. Those two went down below and that was the last I saw of them. I went out on the bridge to be treated by the M.O. but I felt faint through loss of blood and I was taken to the Captain's Sea Cabin just under the bridge and there I remained...The M.O. injected morphine into me and that put me to sleep.

Interestingly, in this account Fred Bean used a euphemism or two and did not tell things exactly as they were, and little wonder. Speaking to Fred's widow and his two sons in 2013, the author heard more details of what actually happened to the two others. Ivor was to one side of Fred, and when the shrapnel sprayed into the caboose, a piece hit Ivor, but it did not hit his ear but his head, and decapitated him. He was killed instantly. Another piece hit Fred on the back of his shoulder, badly wounding him. Another shard hit David Macdonald in the stomach and it was fatal. He died immediately along with Ivor. All through his life Fred had to have his wound cleaned, a wound which never healed properly. David Bean, Fred's son, added to his father's written account:[88]

I was told by my father that all three radar operators were on watch at the start of the enemy engagement. My father told me that he was working the very latest invention, the radar, (RDF 275). He said the radar was so sensitive he could not only see the Admiral Hipper, but also the huge shells being fired from it. After a few salvos the Hipper got the Achates range. I remember my father's exact words, 'They were b.st.rds. They were deadly accurate – by the time they had finished with us our ship was like a pepperpot.

My father then saw a shell fired from the Hipper that was on direct course for the Achates. My father contacted the captain and informed him.

Seconds later the shell landed. It was a direct hit that destroyed the bridge and killed everybody there. I am sorry to say that same shell killed the two radar operators sitting next to my father.

Peyton Jones had an opportunity to count who had died, and the number was more than he had realised. The commander, AHT Jones, was dead along with 40 others. After this attack on the *Achates*, the *Hipper* saw the *Onslow* and the *Orwell* closing, and she altered her course to north, fearing that the two destroyers were going to release torpedoes.

A report was written in 1954 detailing the events which occurred around 11:18 that December morning. It is almost certain Lieutenant Peyton Jones wrote this:[89]

CONFIDENTIAL
ROYAL NAVAL STAFF COLLEGE, GREENWICH
APPENDIX A TO SCHEME NO. 1649
EXTRACTS FROM BATTLE SUMMARY NO. 22
CONVOYS JW51A, JW51B, RA51 DECEMBER, 1942
All Times Zone Minus One (ALFA)

...the HIPPER continued at high speed on course 220°, and at 11:15 engaged the ACHATES, then just clearing her smoke screen in response to orders from Commander Kinloch to join the ONSLOW ahead of the convoy. After three minutes, the ACHATES received a hit which crippled her, killing Lieut. Commander A.H.T. Johns her commanding officer, and some 40 others.

Lieutenant Peyton Jones, who then took command, found he could only overtake the convoy very slowly, so he disregarded his orders and continued to lay smoke as before.

After the explosion, Peyton Jones ran out of the TS and looked up and down the deck of the *Achates*. He saw no damage there. Then, he made for the bridge. At the bottom of the stairway to the bridge, he met a young lad who had been scared witless by the explosion. The lad said that the Yeoman had told him to run for the First Lieutenant.

When Peyton Jones reached the wheelhouse, it was obvious the shell had landed on the bridge from above. There was a ragged hole in the bridge floor with edges bent downwards. The helmsman was in a stupor looking at the destruction around him. Peyton Jones climbed up to the bridge by means of an ack-ack gun platform. There was little left of the stairway to the bridge.

He did not recognise the scene in front of him. Everything was black and burnt – metal, equipment, persons. It was a mercy he could not identify what was left of the bridge personnel.

They were all dead: the Captain, Lieutenant Commander Johns; the *No 2*, Lieutenant Eric Marland; the young Navigator, Sub-lieutenant Kenneth Highfield; the signallers, the lookouts, and the A/S (ASDIC) operators. Permeating everything was the acrid, sour smell of the explosion. Peyton Jones wrote:[90]

Farther aft, the damage was less extensive although still effectively flattened as if by some giant hammer smashing down from above. Here men were lying, not all of them dead. I leant over Fred Barrett, the young sub-lieutenant, who had been directing the gun armament, but he had been too badly wounded to tell me anything.

Peyton Jones climbed over the dead and the devastation, coughing on account of the smoke. He saw the Yeoman, Albert Taylor. It was a miracle he was alive, as everyone around him was dead. Taylor had received several wounds and was still dazed and shaking. However, it was possible for him to relate, albeit haltingly, the last signals between the bridge and the *Obedient*.

Peyton Jones, the new captain, knew that there was one thing he had to put right before he did anything else. The *Achates* was steaming at 28 knots in a circle to starboard and with a 20° list to port. There was only one way to speak to the wheelhouse below and that was to shout down through the ragged hole the *Hipper*'s shell had made through the bridge's deck. The First Lieutenant shouted down to Hall and ordered him to put the wheel to midships to stop the destroyer going in a circle. There was no other person alive in the wheelhouse. The telegraphists' bodies were lying beside their equipment which was now in splinters. Above in the bridge, every instrument was also in fragments, even the compass. Therefore, Peyton Jones was relieved to hear from the coxswain that the steering gear was functioning. The destroyer came round to the south-east, and the list to port lessened. However, the telegraph to the engine room was not working and someone had to run down with orders to them.

The *Hipper* renewed her attack on the *Achates*, straddling her with shells and creating stacks of water. The destroyer immediately altered course to port to dodge the next salvo. At the same time, the new captain ordered a young sailor to run with a message to the gun at the rear of the ship, the only gun which was still working. The order was never carried out. The youth must have been killed by shrapnel from a shell falling close by.

Since Peyton Jones had taken command, smoke had been blinding his eyes. Cordite had caught fire on B gundeck below and he could not see the enemy ship which was firing at him. He assumed it was the *Hipper*.

Suddenly, there was another very close explosion which drove more shrapnel through the side of the ship. The new captain altered course again and sent a message to the engine room to reduce speed to 12 knots. The next time he saw red flashes on the horizon, the shells were heading towards another ship. There was respite for the moment at any rate.

There were other vessels to be seen in the half light and with help from Taylor, the Yeoman, he established who they were. The convoy was about three miles away and sailing south with *Rhododendron*, *Hyderabad*, and *Northern Gem* in their company. To the north-east, there was a group sailing at speed – they believed these were the other British destroyers. He understood from what Taylor said that the *Obedient* was now the flagship and that the *Onslow* had gone to the opposite side of the convoy away from the Germans. To the north there were still flashes of gunfire on the horizon. Peyton Jones could not properly discern what the positions of the vessels signified, but surmised there was still danger from the north. He reckoned that the *Achates* was in a good position to continue laying down smoke to protect the rear of the convoy. He sent an order to the engine room and thick, black, billows belched from the funnel. The *Achates* zig-zagged at the rear of the convoy to conceal the merchant vessels from the enemy.

Lieutenant Peter Wright provided the new captain with a damage assessment when he popped his head and shoulders above the starboard edge of the bridge. He informed Peyton Jones that the shell which had passed through the bridge floor had exploded just underneath, detonating in the sailors' bathroom, and simultaneously obliterating the TS and most of the crew in it.[91]

Peyton Jones also heard that there was damage below the waterline and three or four more compartments were flooding. Worse still there was a considerable hole in the side of the ship beside No. 2 boiler room. They had to close this compartment. Light and power were now absent in many parts of the vessel.

Sub-lieutenant Anthony Davidson came to speak with Peyton Jones and informed him that the fire on B gundeck was extinguished. (In one of *Achates'* zig-zags into the wind, the heavy sea had surged over the forecastle and quenched the flames.) There was a large number of wounded, Davidson reported, and the decks and passageways were filled with them and the dead.[92]

The new captain faced many challenges at just 24 years of age. The vessel was down at the bow and water was flooding into her. She was beginning to go under. In addition to this, there was no sign of Dr MacFarlane. Shortly before this, high explosive shells had been bursting above the *Achates*, and the shrapnel was raining onto the deck. MacFarlane had been running backwards and forwards to the first-aid stations to care for the wounded. It is very likely that the doctor had been swept overboard by the destructive wave of highly compressed air which came from an exploding shell. The doctor had been assiduous in his care of the wounded since the battle had begun.

His medical team continued with their work despite the carnage. It was not an easy task. One of the team, George Barker, had seen a sailor with a piece of shrapnel embedded in his head. He helped another who had been crying out that he couldn't move his legs. He lost consciousness when Barker pulled him out of the debris. The man had lost both legs. Body parts were everywhere.[93]

Time: 11:30

It was 11:30. Peyton Jones had been in charge for only a few minutes. Apart from the heroes who had been caring for the wounded, there were other heroes doing commendable work throughout the ship. In No. 2 boiler room, stoker PO Robert Bell was in charge when a shell exploded near to the *Achates* and penetrated the boiler room. Water started to pour in. He encouraged his crew and started to plug the holes in the side of the ship. He continued to maintain high pressure steam for as long as he could despite the damage in that area. The boiler room lights went out, but Bell continued in the darkness and in the rising cold water, which reached to his waist. He did not leave No. 2 boiler room until ordered to do so.

Kenneth MacIver from Back, Isle of Lewis, hauled several wounded crew members out of a flooding compartment. He helped them get to the medical station, having to run back and forth on a deck which was being showered with shrapnel splinters. After this he went up to what remained of the bridge and to the wheelhouse and took the place of the wounded Hall.

In the W/T (Wireless/Telegraphy) office, William Bartrip was attempting to repair the transmitter and receiver sets in the dark. The telegraphist, Eric Dickenson, was outside trying to set up jury aerials in place of the ones which had been destroyed. Whilst he was attempting the repair, he was hit by a blast of wind from one of *Hipper's* shells. He kept on, though, and completed the work. Whilst the *Achates* was carrying out these repairs, the *Hipper* was making for the convoy like a colossal grey shark.

CHAPTER 27

ADMIRAL BURNETT IN FORCE R

On the *Empire Archer,* Commodore Melhuish was standing on the Monkey Island (the highest bridge on a vessel). Beside him was his Yeoman, Matthews. He received a signal that the *Hipper* was to port. Matthews called down to Madley in the wheelhouse. Madley switched on green and red lights – the order to turn 45° to starboard. Madley switched the lights off – the signal to execute the order – and the merchant vessels executed their fifth emergency turn that morning. They changed course from south-east to due south. The enemy was now to the rear of the convoy.

The *Hipper* had been shelling the three destroyers *Obedient, Obdurate,* and *Orwell,* and in particular the *Obedient,* for six minutes. Suddenly, shells straddled the *Obedient* and shrapnel splinters cut her wireless aerials. Until makeshift jury aerials were rigged, Kinloch could not contact the other destroyers except by signal lamp. Because of this, he transferred command of the task force to Captain Sclater in the *Obdurate.* The signal 'Take charge of destroyers' was sent at 11:39.

Surprisingly, the *Hipper* turned to the west at this moment at 31 knots. When the three destroyers saw this, they turned away and made smoke to protect the convoy. Vice Admiral Kummetz had turned because he was afraid that the destroyers were going to attack using torpedoes.[94] At 11:36, the *Hipper* sent a signal to the *Lützow:*[95]

IN ACTION WITH ESCORTING FORCE. NO CRUISER WITH
THE CONVOY.

However, unknown to Kummetz,[96] Admiral Burnett in Force R had been heading to the field of battle at 30 knots, and the cruisers HMS *Sheffield* and HMS *Jamaica* had now arrived. The *Hipper* had been so occupied with

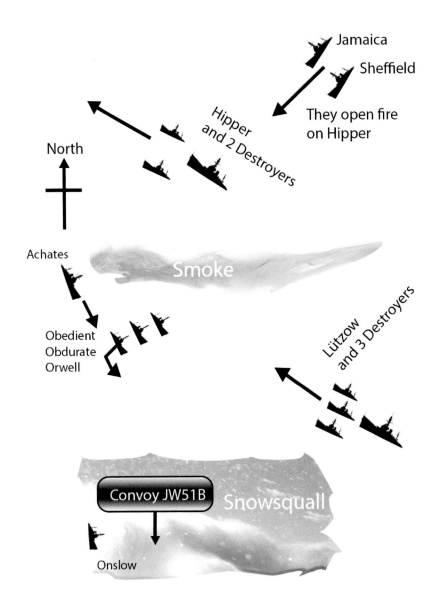

The situation at 11:30 on the morning of 31st December, 1942

the destroyers that they had not been keeping watch on their radar screens. Therefore, when 24 shells fell round about her, the crew were terrified. *Sheffield* and *Jamaica* had fired their 6" guns and had hit the *Hipper* almost immediately. *Hipper* withdrew from the battle, wounded.

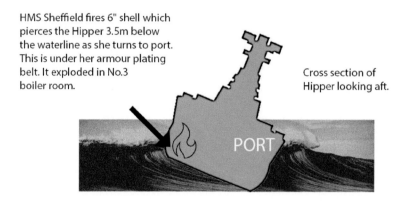

HMS Sheffield fires 6" shell which pierces the Hipper 3.5m below the waterline as she turns to port. This is under her armour plating belt. It exploded in No.3 boiler room.

Cross section of Hipper looking aft.

PORT

Hipper receives two more hits from the Sheffield, the first hits her amidships; the second enters her starboard side, but fails to explode, and continues through to her port side.

PORT

HMS Sheffield fires 6" shell

At the same time, the German destroyer *Eckholdt* came on the scene. No one knew that she had just sunk HMS *Bramble* and that the British minesweeper had gone down with all hands. HMS *Bramble* had been searching for stray convoy vessels when she met with the *Eckholdt* at location 71°18'N 30°06'E.

In only a few minutes, the *Eckholdt* herself would meet the deceased from HMS *Bramble* at the bottom of the ocean. Unfortunately for her, *Eckholdt* thought that the cruisers *Sheffield* and *Jamaica* were German ships and she headed directly towards them. It is not a distortion to say that she was split apart. She was hit midships and broke in two. The German destroyer and all who were in her went down within two minutes. The other German destroyer with her, the *Richard Beitzen*, escaped without harm – 'time and chance happens to all'.

The first salvo from HMS *Sheffield* had straddled the *Hipper*. In the second salvo, fortune favoured the British cruiser. One shell hit the German heavy cruiser just as she was veering to port, and with her starboard side exposed she was holed 3.5m below her waterline, and, therefore, below the armour belt which ran all round her. In subsequent shelling the *Hipper* received two more hits, one setting fire to her aircraft hangar amidships, the other tearing through her starboard side and coming to a halt at the inner wall of the port hull, but without exploding.

The shell which had entered No. 3 boiler room had pierced an oil tank on the way in. When the shell exploded a fire started and water poured in along with the oil from the burst tank. Surprisingly, Engineering Mate, Gunther Walter was the only fatality. He received a head wound and drowned. Another German, Engineering Lance Corporal Heinz Hess, was wounded and taken to a first aid station. The fires were brought under control to an extent with Ardexin fire extinguishers. However, thousands of tons of water had poured into the vessel; they had to close off the boiler room. They had lost the ship's main starboard engine. *Hipper* reduced her speed to 28 knots.[97]

Vice-admiral Kummetz in the *Hipper* was now heading west to meet the *Lützow*. Meanwhile, Captain Stange in the *Lützow* had identified a number of targets through the fog and smoke. The nearest target was three miles away and the furthest merchant vessel seven miles. *Lützow's* guns had a range of 15 miles. None of her salvos from her 11" and 6" guns hit any target. Stange had lost another opportunity – an opportunity which he would not see again. The *Hipper* and Lützow had fired 162 shells between them.[98]

CHAPTER 28

IMPATIENCE AT THE WOLF'S LAIR

Thursday, 31 December, 1942

Time: 11:47

Interestingly, Admiral Kummetz's Operation Regenbögen strategy had worked in one way. The *Hipper* had attracted the attention of the escort force and the convoy. The convoy had altered course to the south and had unknowingly turned into the path of the other claw of the German lobster, the *Lützow*. Convoy JW51B should have experienced a major encounter with the *Kriegsmarine*. However, it appears the German navy did not have sufficient conviction to engage fully with the enemy and destroy the convoy. When he was heading back to Altenfjord, Kummetz wrote in his diary:[99]

> *As we withdrew from the battle scene, it was hard to escape the feeling that, even though the situation appeared to be in our favour, we were unable to get at the convoy, and scored no successes whatsoever.*

At his headquarters in Wolfschanze, Poland, Hitler was waiting impatiently for information about Operation Regenbögen. At 11:47, the submarine *U-354* sent him an ambiguous message relating the great victory Kummetz and his accompanying force had achieved. Kummetz maintained radio silence on the return voyage to Altenfjord. And, after dropping anchor, a misfortune or two delayed his report to Hitler at his headquarters. The Führer did not hear from Kummetz until the afternoon of the following day. In the interval, Hitler had heard on the BBC how two German heavy cruisers had left the field of battle.

Although the Führer himself was to be blamed for limiting and weakening the resolve of his commanders, he excoriated Admiral Krancke, who was liaison officer for the Kriegsmarine in the *OKW (Oberkammando der Wehrmacht Hauptquarier* – The High Command of Nazi Forces). It was bad enough that Regensbögen had failed, but Hitler thought that the delay in the delivery of the message from Kummetz was deliberate and that he was diffident about telling the failures of the Kriegsmarine. Hitler thought this was approaching rebellion.

Admiral Raeder was called to OKW headquarters. He knew what to expect – a badmouthing and the Führer's fury. However, he did not expect the message Hitler gave him. The disparagement lasted an hour and a half. With neck veins bulging and nigh on bursting, Hitler screamed that the German surface navy was useless – and he had been of that opinion for a long time. He also made the accusation that the men and the command were not capable. Therefore, intimated Hitler, the battleships *Tirpitz*, *Schleswig-Holstein*, and *Schlesien*; the heavy cruisers *Admiral Scheer* and *Lützow*; the battlecruisers *Scharnhorst* and *Gneisenau*; the heavy cruisers *Hipper* and *Prinz Eugen*; and the light cruisers *Emden*, *Köln*, *Leipzig* and *Nürnberg* would be decommissioned and broken up. Their guns would be removed and used as coastal batteries.

From this point on, the largest vessel that the Kriegsmarine would have would be a destroyer. Admiral Raeder was ordered to formulate an action plan. Raeder found it difficult to believe what was taking place.

When Raeder returned with a plan, he tried to persuade Hitler to change his mind. He showed Hitler that his plan would only free 300 officers and 8,500 sailors. The metal recovered from the warships would only be sufficient to satisfy Germany's steel demands for one month. He would require 7,000 workers for breaking up the ships, personnel who could be more usefully employed elsewhere in the war effort. In addition, this plan would be of little benefit to the U-boat force. Even if all the steel from dismantling these Kriegsmarine vessels could be used, there would only be sufficient to build seven U-boats per month. As for the guns, it would take a year before they could all be deployed. The 300 officers and the 7,000 sailors who would be freed from the warships would not be suitable for submarine service. Raeder concluded:[100]

I am convinced that the smaller nucleus fleet of destroyers would be unable to accomplish the task assigned to it. The decommissioning of our major assets will hand the enemy a substantial victory at no cost and will be seen by them as a lack of resolve.

Hitler refused to accept Raeder's analysis. Göring, who was in charge of the Luftwaffe, entered the argument. He spoke of the large number of planes which he had deployed simply to guard warships whilst stuck at anchor in Norwegian fjords. These planes could be used more gainfully on the Eastern

Front, he suggested. It did not take Raeder long to realise that Hitler was not going to change his mind, and on 30 January 1943, when Hitler and he were by themselves, he resigned.

It was not a surprise that Admiral Dönitz replaced Raeder. He was ambitious for himself and, importantly to Hitler, in charge of U-boats. Dönitz believed that the U-boats could win the war for Hitler. But, a few months after his appointment, Dönitz was arguing that the *Tirpiz* and the *Scharnhorst* should be kept. This transpired and the other capital ships were also saved.[101]

CHAPTER 29

ON BOARD HMS *ACHATES* AND ON

BOARD HMT *NORTHERN GEM*

Thursday, 31 December, 1942

Time: 13:00

At the same time as the battle was continuing and Force R contending with the Kriegsmarine, Lieutenant Peyton Jones was considering how to mitigate the perilous situation aboard HMS *Achates*. He began to think of another Loftus Peyton Jones, after whom he was named. The first Loftus had been at the Battle of Jutland in the First World War and served as commander of HMS *Shark*. What would he have done in this situation? Peyton Jones confessed that it was thoughts like these which preserved him midst the destruction and death which surrounded him, and prevented him from going into a state of shock or giving in to the horrors all around. He said:[102]

> *I was conscious only of the failing light and increasing cold, wondering what the other destroyers were doing and how it all would end. Slowly, as time passed, the list to port increased and, as it did so, more and more holes, as yet unplugged, were brought below the water line. Eventually, at about 13:00, Peter Wright came up to report that although the fight was still going on, it was no longer possible to maintain steam in Number One boiler, the only one left. Smoke stopped belching from the funnel and Achates wallowed to a halt some three miles on the starboard quarter of the convoy.*
> *"What are you going to do now?" Wright asked me.*

"Get someone to take us in tow," I replied. *"Tell Davidson to prepare to tow aft."*

"We'll do our best," he said with typical cheerfulness as he disappeared from view. *Sadly, that was the last I ever saw of him for he did not survive the sinking. No one could have worked more valiantly to save the ship and his courageous example inspired his shipmates to the very end.*

Taylor, the Yeoman, was operating the box-lamp and signalled the *Northern Gem*, the closest convoy escort boat:

`Not under control. Please stand by me.`

And a little after, he added to the signal:

`Request to be taken in tow.`

However, in a short time Sub-lieutenant Davidson returned to the bridge and informed that it would not be possible to tow the *Achates* because of the angle of her list. Peyton Jones understood immediately that there was now only one course of action, and this was to abandon ship. He ordered Davidson to prepare the lifeboats and the Carley Floats for launching, and to assemble the men on the top deck. Peyton Jones recorded later:[103]

Clambering across the port after-corner of the bridge, I saw that the whaler, still secured in its davits, was already awash and realised just how great were the odds against our remaining afloat. I had become so accustomed to the slowly increasing list that I may already have left things too late, for by now movement around the ship had become very difficult. Many were the acts of bravery performed in getting the more seriously wounded on deck, and some were to pay for this devotion with their lives.

When Yeoman Albert Taylor sent his signal using an old box-lamp, the skipper of the *Northern Gem*, Lieutenant Horace Aithsorpe, had difficulty understanding it in the misty half-light. At first, he thought it was the enemy who was signalling, and he kept his converted trawler at a distance from the supposed enemy vessel lest it be a *ruse de guerre*.[104]

Box-Lamp

The rescue ship HMT *Northern Gem* departing Hvalfjord, Iceland

On board the *Achates*, the Bridge did not understand why the rescue ship was standing off, and Peyton Jones asked the Yeoman to resend the signal. The Yeoman had only sent a few words when the destroyer began slowly to roll onto its side. With assurance now that it was not an enemy vessel, the *Northern Gem* sailed closer to the *Achates*. This is how the coxswain of the *Northern Gem*, Sydney A Kerslake, recollected the incident:[105]

> ...we were told that the Achates was in a bad way, and was in no condition to be towed, and that we were going to stand by her. Rescue nets were put over the port side, and heaving lines were got ready; those of our crew who were not doing essential work were positioning themselves along the full length of the port side as we came up on the starboard side of the stricken Achates. She certainly seemed in a bad way, from what I could see of her as both ships were being lifted on the top of the heavy broken swell. She looked well down by the stern and had a great list over to port.

As the trawler drew close, the *Achates* capsized. She was like a huge whale turning in the water for the last time. Some of the *Achates'* crew had assisted Sub-lieutenant Anthony Davidson in cutting the ropes which secured the Carley Floats and the rafts – the rafts were nets of thick rope with cork floats.

Sailors inspecting a Carley float

The angle of the ship meant that it would be difficult to climb the stairways below deck. When the order was given for every man to make for the highest deck, some ran below to the Sick Bay to save the wounded. The injured would not be able to climb the stairways by themselves and would have to be hauled up from below. There were some who could not be moved and Drummond, the canteen manager, and Alan Jones, the Steward, chose to remain with them, even although they knew that the vessel was about to go under.

While the work of rescuing the wounded was going on, PO Telegraphist Bartripp was visiting the bridge, the wheelhouse, and the wireless office to make certain that all the secret documents (cyphers, orders, and reference books) were locked in the safe so that they would not float to the surface and be picked up by the Germans.

The *Achates* was sinking. Her port side – which was like a colander because of shrapnel damage – was almost submerged. The sea was pouring in through the funnel and the hatches to the decks below. Drummond and Jones were trapped along with the wounded, whom they had not forsaken. All were drowned.

On the bridge, Peyton Jones and Taylor were attempting to climb onto the side of the wheelhouse, which was now parallel with the icy seawater. They looked

Canteen Manager
George Albert Drummond

down through its open door. Inside were two sailors struggling to save themselves. One of them was Sub-lieutenant Barret, who had been badly wounded, the other Able Seaman Kenneth MacIver from the Isle of Lewis. Peyton Jones described the situation:

Looking down into the wheelhouse passage at our feet I saw Fred Barrett being helped by Able Seaman MacIver out of the captain's sea cabin and, reaching down, we hauled them up beside us.

Most of the wounded were sitting or lying on the side of the boat – a situation which did not last for long. Peyton Jones thought that it was time for him to remove the encumbrance of his binoculars from around his neck. He had barely hung them on a protrusion before the *Achates* capsized:[106]

I recall having time to unsling my binoculars from around my neck and hang them carefully on some convenient projection before the ship completed her capsize and the sea surged over our heads. The water, needless to say, was bitterly cold, only one degree I believe above freezing, but it took a moment or two to penetrate my many layers of clothing and I struck out to get clear of the ship. Looking back, I saw the dark outline of her screws and rudder as she slowly disappeared, stern pointing to the sky, and felt a sudden stab of sorrow at this sad end to so much endeavour.

The *Achates* had sunk so quickly that she dragged many down with her, amongst them the engineer Peter Wright, and Kenneth MacIver who a few minutes before had been rescued from the wheelhouse.

In the turmoil, Peyton Jones lost sight of his companions from the wheelhouse. But he did notice that many Carley Floats and rafts had been loosed from the ship and mentally gave thanks to Davidson and his team for their work. One of the floats was close to him and he swam towards it and clambered aboard.

Fred Bean, the only person who had escaped from the radar station alive, had been asleep for several hours due to the morphine injection he had been given. This is his account of his final minutes aboard the *Achates*:[107]

I was taken to the Captain's Sea Cabin just under the Bridge and there I remained for five hours unconscious. The M.O. injected morphine into me and that put me to sleep. The next thing I remembered was when the ship listed right over to port and I was thrown out of my bunk. I wondered what had happened until I saw the water filling the cabin. I waded through the water and up onto the Gun Deck. I had a hard job to climb up there. At one time, I thought I was trapped… a ladder stopped me from getting up. And the water came, coming higher and higher. Oh boy, was I scared.

…I managed to get my gammy arm working and clawed my way onto the Gun Deck. The position of the ship was right over, 90 degrees, and she was speedily sinking bows first. I had to work fast. I was still feeling rather dazed after the morphine injection. I had only enough strength to get my head and shoulders onto the Gun Deck. I shouted for the 1st Lieutenant [Peyton Jones] who was waiting to jump into the water. He came up to me and helped me up. By this time, we were knee deep in water. There were three other chaps on the Gun Deck as well. To our luck a Carley Float just passed about 5 yards away from where I was standing. One of the chaps jumped for it and landed…I thought what he could do I can do. So, I jumped, but not into it. I just managed to grab hold of the float. Jimmy The One [Peyton Jones] was the next to jump and he made it. When he was in, he helped me into the float. By the time I was settled down, there was about five men on the float, and about 6 hanging around it, doing the crawl with their free hand, and as luck was with us we drifted towards the Northern Gem (armed trawler) which was about 75 yards away.

I turned around just in time to see the ship's bows disappearing. She must have turned on her even keel while sinking. For she was going down at about 45 degrees, and she went quite quickly. During all this period, it was dark and you could only see about 100 yards. While going towards the trawler, we all sang 'You are my Sunshine', not 'Roll Out the Barrel' as the papers stated. [This contradicts the recollection of other sailors.] By the time the song was finished, we had quite a crowd hanging on around the float, and a few chaps got into it. It was then I noticed the Coxswain trying his utmost to get the float towards the trawler and he made a good job of it.

When we arrived at the ship's side, which took about a quarter of an hour all told, we saw another float alongside and quite a number of chaps treading water and waiting to be hauled up… a few more strung onto the float. There was a little panic for the first time, but that was soon got under control. Well, then our float turned turtle and in I went again. Then all the lines came over the side [of the Northern Gem] and most of the chaps went to the ship's side and got on board. But, I stuck to the float until the panic died down. There was only 3 chaps in the float by this time and I was the only one hanging on. I asked the Signal Officer if he would lift me in, but he said he was too weak. So, I asked

Lieutenant Horace Aisthorpe
HMT *Northern Gem*

Jimmy The One again and once more he gave me a hand and I got into the float. Later the Signal Officer died on board with shrapnel in his stomach–tough luck.

On board the *Northern Gem*, the skipper, Lieutenant Horace Aisthorpe, was keeping an eye on the *Achates*. He wrote:

As we waited there we watched her turn keel up, and then the men started jumping off and making their way as best they could toward us.

He heard someone singing 'Roll Out the Barrel' and within a few minutes others of the *Achates*' crew were singing it as well:[108]

Here they were in dire peril, not only from drowning, but freezing to death if we could not get them out of the water within a few minutes, singing at the tops of their voices. Those who had survived the action and the struggle to keep their ship the Achates afloat, were now fighting for their own lives, to save themselves in those cold and freezing waters of the stormy Arctic Ocean.

When the men from the *Achates* hit the water with the red lights on their lifejackets activated, the rescuers on the *Northern Gem* could see a myriad will-o'-the-wisps bobbing amongst the white caps of the Barents Sea. Here and there were stronger white lights from the Carley Floats. It was like a scene from a perverse winter fairyland.

Kerslake, coxswain of the rescue ship, succeeded in hauling one survivor on board. He saw another man, a young lad, drifting past the stern of the boat with his hand outstretched, looking for a rope which he hoped someone would throw to him. Kerslake threw one, and the rope fell over the shoulders of the young lad. But the young man was benumbed and he could not feel the rope on his shoulders. Kerslake shouted at him to get a hold of the rope, but he could not move his arms. Next, Kerslake tried to loop the rope around the boy's shoulders, but he did not succeed. In his final moments, Kerslake heard the boy crying out for his mother, and the word '*Mother!*' was the last utterance Kerslake heard from the boy before he drowned. Kerslake himself wept through frustration and helplessness. Following this event, he recorded what happened next:[109]

Just at that precise moment, there was a terrific underwater explosion, and the Northern Gem was lifted bodily out of the water. The surface of the sea shivered for a few moments then burst into a boiling cauldron of confused froth. When it returned to its former state, there was no one left alive in the water, there were probably six or eight bodies floating past, still with their life-jackets on, on which glowed the red lights, but there was no sign of any life; they had either been killed by the explosion, or had succumbed to the frightful cold of the water. Our CO then thought it wise to go onto full speed to catch up with the convoy as the German surface vessels as far as he knew were still lurking in the area, and the Gem wasn't built to fight a ship-to-ship battle of that sort.

The *Northern Gem* was now travelling at full speed in rough seas. Kerslake went down below to put on dry clothing. Then he visited every survivor who had been pulled from the water. He gave each a good measure of rum to promote their blood circulation. There were around a dozen who required a doctor but there was not a doctor on board. Amongst the dozen was Bartlett, a young sub-lieutenant, who was uncomplaining, but in danger of losing his life because of internal injuries. Kerslake described the condition of others who could look after themselves:[110]

Those survivors who were able helped themselves to towels, dried their bodies and rubbed their limbs briskly to bring back some life to them, then climbed into bunks, and were wrapped in warm blankets; I made certain that I missed no one with the rum jar. As the circulation gradually came back to the limbs of many of these men, some were screaming with pain, a pain which must have been excruciating. Our lads were doing their best to alleviate this by massage, followed by covering them with warm blankets or clothing brought up from the store of survivors' clothes. After some time the sounds of the men in pain gradually died away as they lapsed into various depths of sleep.

The plight of the wounded was of grave concern. There was only one person amongst the rescue ship's crew who had any rudimentary medical knowledge. This was Eric Mayer, a sailor 40 years of age who had worked in a bank before the war started. His wife was a nurse and he had a friend who was a doctor. Mayer had basic knowledge through these contacts, but he could only clean and disinfect wounds.

Kerslake described how he came into contact with Peyton Jones when he was doing his rounds:[111]

He was sat in the forward mess-deck, very concerned about his crew, though he realised that we were doing our best. I apologised for the fact that he had

*been taken to the seamen's mess, and conducted him to the wardroom to join
the other three surviving officers where he was greeted warmly by them and
our own officers who were present. They had all thought him to be lost with the
ship, and the surprise and pleasure on their faces when I took him in was good
to see after the happenings of the last few hours.*

Peyton Jones wanted to bring a doctor on board the *Northern Gem* as quickly
as possible. The skipper, Horace Aisthorpe, was of the same opinion. He could
only guess where the convoy might be now. He kept on at full speed, hoping that
he was on the correct course. At one point, they saw HMS *Obedient* go past their
stern. They initially took fright, because they thought it was a German vessel.
Aisthorpe managed to send a signal by Aldis Lamp to the *Obedient* despite the
snowsquall and discovered he was on the correct course for rejoining the convoy.

When the *Achates* went
down, she was approximately
240 miles north-west of the
Kola Inlet. She had sailed
2,410 miles (90%) of the
2,653 miles of her intended
journey between Gourock
and Murmansk. The first
of the *Hipper's* shells had
straddled her at 09:41, with
a later salvo at 11:15. In the
two engagements, 40 of the
crew had been killed. David
Macdonald from Skye
was lost in the latter set of
salvoes. When the *Achates*
went down at 14:00, 70
more of the crew were
killed, including Kenneth

Aldis Lamp coated in ice

MacIver from Lewis. Thirty of the 70 lost at this time had been below deck and
so badly wounded they could not be moved. Others were lost on account of the
ice-cold sea, or the final explosion, or their wounds. Out of a crew of 193, 110
were lost.

The *Northern Gem* rescued 83 souls.

CHAPTER 30

NEW YEAR'S DAY, 1943

Friday, 1 January, 1943

The *Northern Gem* moved to the rear of the convoy for the night and it was there she welcomed in New Year's Day, 1943. At midday, she received the order to sail to the *Obdurate* to take a doctor on board. The wounded from the *Achates* were in dire need of medical attention. The sea state was so rough and the weather so ferocious that they could not lower a tender.

Aisthorpe, the skipper, came into the wheelhouse and said:

Right, Cox, I'll take her.

He had decided to take the trawler up to the *Obdurate* and ordered the crew to get fenders ready to come alongside. Slowly, the *Northern Gem* edged towards the port side of the destroyer. Both vessels were manoeuvering very carefully during this dangerous operation. In the grey half-light they saw a small group at the stern of the *Obdurate*, and one person with a rope around his middle. This was Maurice Hood. He was going to endanger his life to provide medical assistance for the *Achates'* wounded. On the *Northern Gem* a small group of officers and crew were waiting to catch Hood when he jumped.

When there was a lull in the weather, Aisthorpe moved the bow of the 57m trawler nearer to the side of the 105m destroyer. When there was just a foot or two between the two vessels, the skipper turned the wheel to port and the *Northern Gem* moved close enough to give Hood an opportunity to jump. The two ships came together for a second. This gave the doctor his opportunity to leap seven or eight feet down onto the deck of the trawler. It was a hero's leap.

A doctor was on board at last.

The surgeon went below with his Gladstone bag and began to treat the injured sailors, a process which had to be carried out under conditions which were exceedingly dangerous. Peyton Jones described the scene:[112]

There were some horrific wounds and several operations were needed to repair the damaged bones and flesh. At his request, I administered the anaesthetic, slowly dripping chloroform on to a face mask or emptying a syringe into a vein as he directed, whilst Mayer handed him his instruments. On the wildly gyrating deck, all three of us had to be anchored round the waist by two men each, so that we could have both hands free. Someone held a specially bright torch to illuminate the work, whilst two more held the patient stretched out on one of the wooden mess tables. Never, I think, can surgery have been conducted under more difficult conditions, and I marvelled at the Doctor's cool competence and skill. I marvelled, too, at the courage of these badly wounded men whose stoic determination alone had enabled them to survive.

I think there were some twelve cases in all, and we worked thus all day. The doctor thought everyone would recover except for poor Freddie Barrett, for whom he could hold out little hope and who died uncomplainingly that night.

CHAPTER 31

SOME RESPITE

Saturday, 2 January, 1942

The next morning, the *Northern Gem,* received permission to stop and hold a burial service for the young Sub-lieutenant, Fred Barrett. All from the *Achates* who were not wounded, gathered on the deck, with every available crew member of the *Northern Gem.* Aisthorpe gave the ship's prayer book to Peyton Jones. It was evident that the book had been well used. The young First Lieutenant read the solemn words:

> *We therefore commit his body to the deep, to be turned into corruption, looking for the resurrection of the body, (when the Sea shall give up her dead,) and the life of the world to come, through our Lord Jesus Christ; who at his coming shall change our vile body, that it may be like his glorious body, according to the mighty working, whereby he is able to subdue all things to himself.*

The words from the order of service for the funeral made an impact on each person present as they remembered the 109 others who were lost from the *Achates.* Each one was remembered as a friend and a hero.

At the rising of the sun, the *Northern Gem* glimpsed land and at 10:15 the convoy altered course again.[113] At 13:00 the section of the convoy which was going to Archangel separated from the other two columns and continued further along the coast. At 17:40 Kildin Island was spotted on the route into the Kola Inlet and the *Obedient* and the *Rhododendron* went to the south of the convoy to rendezvous with the pilot boat. At 23:00 Convoy JW51B altered course again to 226° and headed down the Kola Inlet. The wind had dropped to Force 2.

Kola Inlet and Murmansk with Archangel (Arkhangelsk) to the east

Sunday, 3 January, 1943

Between 05:00 and 09:00 each merchant vessel, apart from three, had tied up to the pier in Murmansk. The merchant vessels *Calobre*, *Vermont*, and *Pontfield* were missing. HMS *Obedient* located the *Vermont* in the Kildin Straight, and a short while after this spotted the *Calobre* on her way into Murmansk, and the *Vizalma* in her company. This meant that each one of the 14 merchant vessels in Convoy JW51B had reached the Kola Inlet safely, although the *Pontfield* went aground inside the Inlet and was towed to Rosta drydock. The SS *Ballot* ran aground near the shores of Kildin Island in fog on 2 January and was abandoned by her crew on 13 January. (Another report suggested she was torpedoed.)[114]

The *Northern Gem* berthed at a quay in Vaenga beside the *Onslow* which had gone ahead of the convoy so that her wounded could receive medical attention. The wounded from the *Achates* were hospitalised here also. The level of care in the hospital was not of a high standard. It was an ordinary building which had been altered to accommodate the wounded. Therefore, it had neither equipment, nor heat, nor light as it ought to have had. Fortunately, there were two surgeons from the Royal Navy in it who did the best they could. Maurice Hood, who had already done so much for the *Achates'* wounded, came ashore to help them. His assistance was invaluable in the hospital at Vaenga.

Peyton Jones visited his crew who were in the hospital, and he also called on

Captain Sherbrooke who had been badly wounded in the face and had lost an eye. A few days after this, news came that Sherbrooke had been awarded the Victoria Cross. No one disputed the award. All thought him worthy because of what he had accomplished with his small task force against an enemy which had been much stronger. Admiral Tovey wrote:

> *That an enemy force of one pocket battleship, one heavy cruiser and six destroyers, with all the advantages of surprise and concentration, should be held off for four hours by five destroyers and driven from the area by two 6inch gun cruisers, is most creditable and satisfactory.*

Captain Sherbrook replied to Tovey's signal:

```
Your signal is much appreciated. This Award is a
tribute to the force in general and I hope will
be taken by the next of kin of those who lost
their lives, as some measure of their country's
appreciation.
```

There was little respite from the war in the Kola Inlet, though. That night, the Germans dropped incendiary bombs on Vaenga (now Severomorsk and is 16 miles northeast of Murmansk) and Murmansk port. Although a fire or two started on land, none of the vessels was badly damaged. However, the air attacks on the port of Murmansk through the day slowed down the unloading of cargo.

CHAPTER 32

SAFE HOME

Monday, 11 January, 1943

A decision was made about the wounded. The very badly injured were to return home on the *Obedient*, amongst whom was Captain Sherbrooke and most of *Achates'* survivors. On 11th January, the *Obedient* sailed on her own and reached Scapa Flow inside five days. The First Lord of the Admiralty, A. V. Alexander, and Admiral Tovey came on board. They commended Peyton Jones. The wounded were transferred to a hospital ship. Peyton Jones and the other survivors continued to Leith. Following this, Peyton Jones returned to Gourock where he learned that he was to travel to Liverpool to meet the Commander-in-Chief, Western Approaches, Admiral Sir Max Horton.

In Liverpool, Horton showed Peyton Jones the signal he had received from Commander-in-Chief Home Fleet, Admiral Tovey. The signal was distributed to every wounded sailor and to close relatives of those involved:[115]

```
A study of the reports now received on the recent
action in the Barent Sea makes it clear that the
Achates played a most valiant part and that the
smokescreen she made to cover the convoy and which
she continued to make almost up to the time of
sinking in spite of having received heavy damage,
contributed greatly to the safety of the convoy
until our reinforcements arrived. We in the Home
Fleet deeply regret the loss of a fine ship and so
many gallant officers and men.
```

Sir Max Horton also wanted Peyton Jones to see a signal he had received from Rear Admiral Robert Burnett from Vice-Admiral Golovko, Commander-in-Chief, North Russian Fleet:[116]

The following message which has just been received from Vice-Admiral Golovko, Commander-in-Chief, North Russian Fleet, is forwarded. The loss of Achates when serving with the Home Fleet Destroyers was deeply regretted and her gallant action was an inspiration to all who were in company with her:

I congratulate you upon your victory over the enemy. You withstood a battle against superior forces, and, despite the latter's counter action, brought the convoy in its entirety into our waters. I sincerely regret the loss of the destroyer Achates and of its valiant company.

Admiral Burnett who had been in the *Sheffield*, and in command of Force R in the Barents Sea, considered that the *Achates* had played a major part in the engagement. Peyton Jones visited the families of each officer who had been killed in the battle. He also wrote to the families of each sailor who had been lost in the conflict. Amongst them were the families of David Macdonald and Kenneth MacIver. The letters Peyton Jones wrote have been kept by the families:

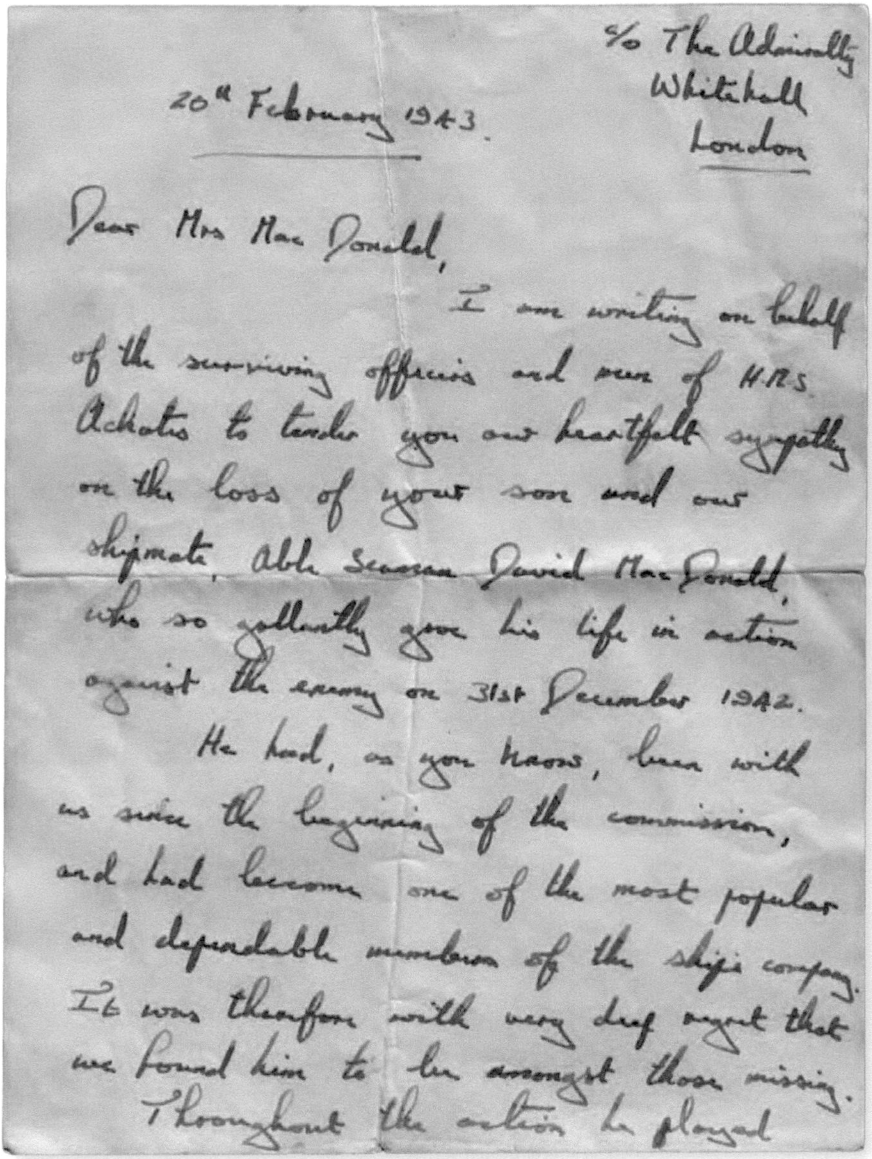

20ᵗʰ February 1943.

c/o The Admiralty
Whitehall
London

Dear Mrs Mac Donald,

I am writing on behalf of the surviving officers and men of H.M.S. Achates to tender you our heartfelt sympathy on the loss of your son and our shipmate, Able Seaman David Mac Donald, who so gallantly gave his life in action against the enemy on 31st December 1942.

He had, as you know, been with us since the beginning of the commission, and had become one of the most popular and dependable members of the ship's company. It was therefore with very deep regret that we found him to be amongst those missing.

Throughout the action he played

his post manfully and well and remained at his post to the end. You may well feel very proud of him.

It ever in the future I can be of any assistance to you, please do not hesitate to let me know. I shall be only too glad to do anything I can.

Yours very sincerely,

L. E. Peyton Jones.

Lieutenant R. N.

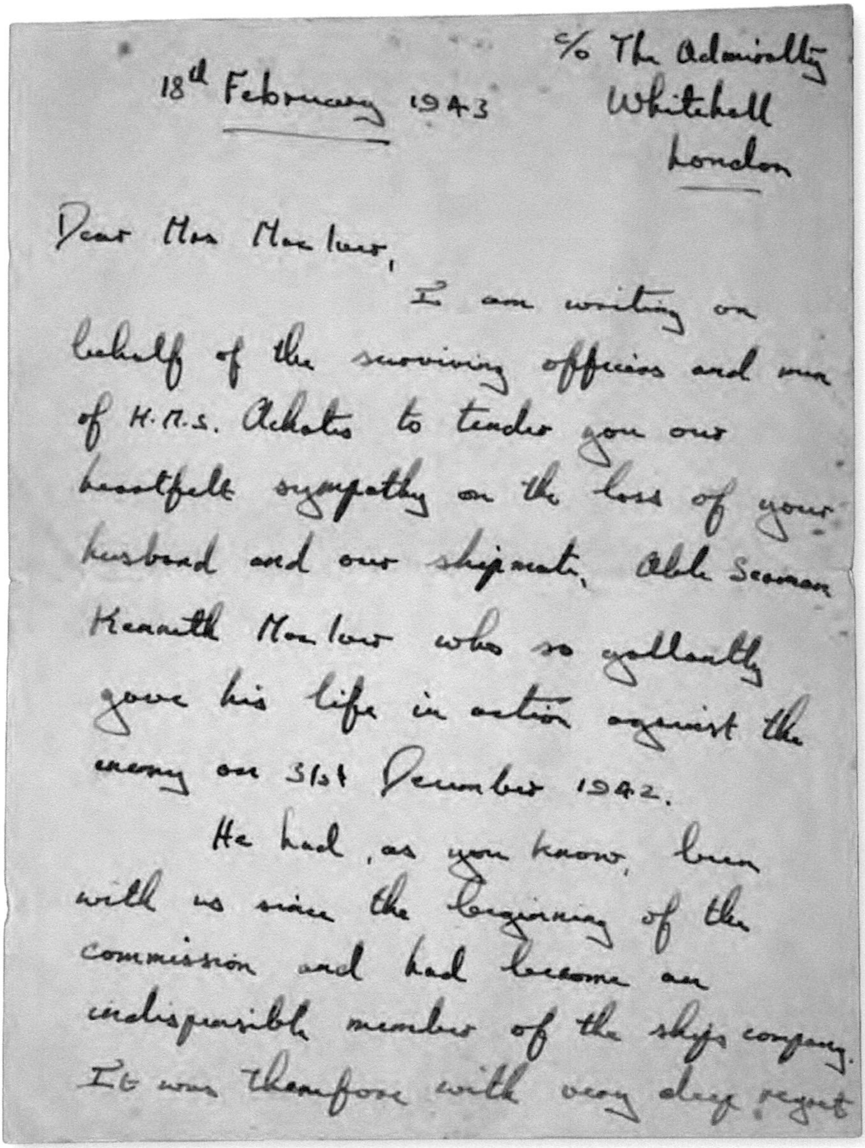

c/o The Admiralty
Whitehall
London

18th February 1943

Dear Mrs MacIver,

I am writing on behalf of the surviving officers and men of H.M.S. Achates to tender you our heartfelt sympathy on the loss of your husband and our shipmate, Able Seaman Kenneth MacIver who so gallantly gave his life in action against the enemy on 31st December 1942.

He had, as you know, been with us since the beginning of the commission and had become an indispensible member of the ship's company. It was therefore with very deep regret that we found him to be amongst those missing.

Throughout the action he worked unceasingly, entirely regardless of his own safety, and I cannot speak too highly of the fine example of courageous devotion to duty which he set his shipmates. — He was indeed a man among men and you may well feel most proud of him.

If ever in the future I can be of any assistance to you please do not hesitate to let me know. I shall be only too glad to do anything I can.

Yours very sincerely,

R. E. Peyton Jones.
Lieutenant R.N.

CHAPTER 33

CONCLUSION

The strategy of the Germans had been a puzzle to many, especially to Commander Kinloch. He noted:[117]

> *The inactivity of the German destroyers is inexplicable. They made no attack on the convoy and in two engagements were following astern of their cruiser without taking any part.*

Many of those who survived considered that a favourable providence was the reason for convoy JW51B's safe arrival: the onset of a snowsquall around 10:45, which hid the convoy from the Lützow and its task force when they intended initiating an attack, undoubtedly preserved the convoy at that time. Captain Stange did not realise how close he had been to achieving success.

The recollection of 18 year old Midshipman Albert Twiddy represented the thoughts of many others. (Twiddy would later be promoted to Lieutenant Commander.) He was on HMS *Sheffield* and he saw the German destroyer *Friedrich Eckholdt* and her crew being consigned to the bottom of the sea – an image which remained with him for the rest of his life. As 1942 drew to a close, he was certain that it was God alone who had preserved his ship, his friends, and his own life.[118]

It was also clear that Captain Sherbrooke and Commander Kinloch saw it as their duty to protect the convoy, come what may. Sherbrooke also knew that the Germans were afraid of torpedo attacks. Therefore, he did not permit the close protection destroyers to be drawn away from the convoy. Despite the large German task force, the small Royal Navy task force drove the Kriegsmarine away time after time, after which the British destroyers returned to their convoy position.

Commodore Melhuish departed Kola Inlet on 29 January on SS *Daldroch* with a cargo of cotton and wood. There were 11 merchant ships in the return convoy RA52, with 21 Royal Navy vessels protecting them. (Why had he not returned in the *Empire Archer?* – some are of the opinion that the engine room had been so badly damaged when the Barlinnie prisoners had gone on the rampage that repairs had to be made before she could return home.) Melhuish and RA52 arrived in Loch Ewe on February 9, with the loss of one boat, SS *Greylock*, which had been sunk by *U-255* on 3 February.[119]

Between August 1941 and May 1945, 78 convoys sailed to the Arctic. This involved 1,400 vessels. The convoys to the Arctic delivered more than 4 million tons of war supplies. Eighty-five merchant vessels and 16 Royal Navy warships (two cruisers, six destroyers, and eight other escort ships) had been sunk. More than 3,000 sailors and service men lost their lives in the convoys to Russia.

On the German side, losses are estimated to be one battleship and three destroyers, 31 U-boats, and an unrecorded number of planes. It is not certain how many Germans lost their life. The Russians lost at least 29 merchant vessels in the convoys and many warships, planes, and wounded.

Although there were more losses in the Atlantic Convoys, there was more likelihood that a sailor and his ship would be lost on the journey to Russia than any other journey during the Second World War.

We shall leave the final word with Admiral of the Fleet, Lord Tovey, GCB, KBE, DSO, Commander-in-Chief, Home Fleet 1940-1943:[120]

The Battle of the Barents Sea was one of the finest examples in either of the two World Wars of how to handle destroyers and cruisers in action with heavier forces. Captain Sherbrooke saved his convoy by going straight in to attack his far heavier enemy, using his guns to do what damage they could but relying on his torpedoes, the real menace to the heavy ships, to deter them from closing the convoy.

Sherbrooke knew the threat was lost once his torpedoes were fired. When in position for firing he turned his ships to simulate an attack – the mere threat was sufficient to persuade the enemy to break off their attack…

As Sherbrooke went in to attack, the Commodore turned his convoy away and it was quickly covered by smoke from the Achates. Throughout the action the Commodore handled his convoy with great skill…

Smoke-laying may not appear a very exciting way of fighting but I know few things more unpleasant than being fired at when you cannot shoot back. Apart from preventing the enemy getting a sight of the convoy, there is always the chance of a torpedo attack developing out of the smoke. The sinking of the smoke-layer is essential if the enemy is to get a chance of damaging the convoy and the Achates was constantly coming under fire, but she stuck to her job right up to the time she sank – truly a noble little ship and company.

Appendices

Appendix 1

Loftus Peyton Jones at Royal Naval school and in 1943

Peyton Jones at Royal Naval school,
Dartmouth

Piping group, Dartmouth

Refectory, Dartmouth

Photograph of Lt. Peyton Jones taken
in February 1943 after the sinking of
HMS *Achates*

Lieutenant Loftus Peyton Jones in 1945

Appendix 2

Report by Loftus Peyton Jones on the loss of the *ACHATES*
(from the Peyton Jones family collection)

Loss of the Achates.   1.

At about 0920,Thursday,31st December, gun flashes were seen astern
of the convoy.The ship's company were piped to action stations
stations and the 3rd boiler connected. Shortly afterwards an enemy rep
-ort of three destroyers was received from Obdurate and Achates
altered course and speed as necessary to screen the convoy with
smoke in accordance with previous instructions.

Almost immeddiately the ship was straddled,and at about 0945   e
a very near miss on the port side holed the forward shell room,magazin
and stokers' messdeck,and shrapnel caused casualties among the
port Oerlikon guns crew and bridge personnel.This shell also put
the Type 271 out of action.

An attempt was made to close the magazine and shell room
hatches and plug the holes in the stokers messdeck,but it was found
that both strongbacks had been lost in the explosion,and by the
time those door belonging to the after magazine had been sent for
the whole messdeck had had to be abandoned. Efforts were made
to pump out the magazine and shell room by steam ejectors but it
was discovered the steam line had been shattered.

The portable pump electric pump was then brought forward
and a start made on pumping out the half-flooded messdeck,but
after 20 minutes it was apparent that no progess was being made.The
messdeck was therefore closed down and the hatches and forward
and after bulkheads shored up.
                                    between decks
Meanwhile all hands/were employed plugging the innumerable
small holes in the ship's side on the forward messdeck,though this
work was inevitably impeded by first having to clear away the
lagging.

The portable electric pump was moved aft to keep the water
down in the ERAs and Stoker POs messes which were slowly filling,
but an electrical fault on the pump connection held up this
operation for about 20 minutes.

The Downton suction line was employed pumping out the forward
lower messdeck,which was also holed on the port side and which
started filling slowly as the ship trimmed down by the head.

Meanwhile Achates continued her role of smoke-layer until
at 1110 she was ordered by Obedient to prolong the line to port.
On informing the SO that she was damaged and her maximimum speed reduce
to 20 knots, a further signal was received to"proceed to the head
of the convoy and to take Onslow under your orders".

This she proceed ef to do but at about 1115 again came under
accurate enemy fire and in spbte of increasing speed and zigzagging,
received a direct hit on the fore end of the bridge which killed
or seriously wounded all the bridge and wheelhouse personnel,except
the Yeoman (Albert W.Taylor) and Coxswain (CPO Daniel Hall),and
put B gun and its crew out of action. A cordite fire was started
on B gun deck but was soon put out by seas which came over the
foredeck as the ship turned into the wind.

On arrival on the bridge a few minutes later I found the
ship circling to starboard under 20 degrees of wheel and doing 28
knots,giving her a 20 degree list to port.All the bridge and wheelhous
instruments had been wrecked,but the wheel and engineroom telegraphs
remained undamaged.

Loss 2

Speed was reduced to 12 knots in order to bring the damaged port side higher out of the water, and the ship steadied on a mean course roughly parallel with the convoy.

The engine-room was ordered verbally to recommence making smoke, and as it was not considered desirable to exceed a speed of 12 knots until the damage had been fully brought under under control, Obedient's last signal was disregarded and the ship conned as requisite to keep the convoy screened with smoke.

A new crew was formed for B gun but it was found impossible to move the gun in training and they were dispersed. No communication could be established with Y gun, and although a verbal message was sent ordering them to open fire on the enemy, then bearing on the port quarter, it never reached them. A few minutes later the enemy was lost to view.

The ship was straddled on two more occasions before the firing ceased and received a dd direct hit in the seamen's bathroom, port side, and a near miss abreast No. 2 boiler room.

The former hit put the TS out of action and killed most of the crew. It also fractured the after bulkhead of the now-flooded Stokers' messdeck and penetrated the ship's side abreast the ERAs and Stoker POs messes, necessitating the shutting down of these and the Torpedomen's messdecks and resulting in the flooding of the Lowx Power Room. This caused a temporary failure of lighting and power forward, but emergency leads were run from aft and in the meantime all secondary lighting functioned correctly.

The near miss abreast No 2 boiler room caused large holes in the ship's side and this boiler room became flooded and was abandoned.

No.1 boiler room was also holed, but not seriously, and the water was kept under control by the steam ejector. This damage was not reported to the bridge until some time later.

The ship had by this time taken up a 15 degree list to port, and being down by the head became difficult to steer. With the aid of a boat's compass in the wheelhouse she was however kept steaming across the stern and starboard quarter of the convoy, and endevours were made to keep the smoke laid between it and the convoy.

Gun flashes could still be seen to the north and north-west. At 1145 Hyderabad was asked by V/S whether the smoke screen was still effective and of value and reported to the effect that it was most useful. "Damaged, 12 knots" was made by V/S to the only destroyer visible about this time.

About 1200 a signal was received from Sheffield "Report Situation". Being unable to transmit, even from the emergency set, a V/S signal was made to what was thought to be the Hyderabad and subsequently turned out to be Northern Gem, asking to her to pass to Sheffield :"One boiler room and forward lower compartments flooded. Bridge out of action. 15 degree list. Maximum speed 12 knots. About 30 casualties including captain killed." This signal was subsequently cancelled and never transmitted.

Loss 3

Meanwhile all spare hands were put under the orders of the
Engineer Officer for work on damage control.The situation,though
serious, was not then considered critical,but the port list
gradually increased and,as it did so, more and more holes in the
ship's side,as yet unplugged,were submerged,until at 1300 it was
no longer possible to maintain steam in No 1 boiler room and the
ship was stopped.She was then about 3 miles on the starboard side
of the convoy.

"Not under control.Please stand by me" was made to Northern Gem
at 1300,and preparations were made for the ship to be taken in
tow from aft. The list to port continued to increase however
until the upper deck was awash and the order given to clear away
boats and rafts and all men ordered on the upper deck.

Consideration was given to firing torpedoes set to safe and
jettisoning ready use ammunition in order to reduce top weight,but
it was decided that these measures would not appreciably improve
the ship s stability.

A hasty check was made that no CBs or SPs were left on the
bridge or in the wheelhouse and it was confirmed that those in the
wheelhouse were locked in the steel chest provided.

A signal was commenced to Northern Gem asking her to take the
ship in tow aft,but was never completed as the ship rolled alarmingly
to port until she lay on her beam ends. Achates sunk at 1300 about
1300 in approximate position 73 03 North, 30 42 East.

All Carley floats and rafts from the starboard side were got
away and a few of those from the port side subsequently floated
to the surface.

Northern Gem stopped about half a cable on the starboard beam
and in spite of the semi-darkness and considerable swell succeeded
in picking up 81 survivors.

Orders had been given to remove all depthcharge primers   from
depth charges early in the action,but it subsequently transpired
that three or four had so iced up as to be immovable and these
exploded some £ 35 minutes after the ship sank.No more survivors
were then visible from Northern Gem,and it is not considered that
this explosion caused any further loss of,life.

Remarks : Enemy fire appeared very accurate for line but
the ex spread for range averaged 400 yards.Near misses caused more
extensive damage to the hull than the actual hits.All were HE shells
and burst on impact.

All ice on the upper deck and superstructure had been cleared
away the day before and it is not considered that stability was
affected. Low temperatures and the fact men were wounded before
ever they entere the water undoubtedly contributed to the large
loss of life.Approximately x 40 were killed in action before the
ship sank......
                    Sgd L.P-J.

List of Officers and Ratings and Comments
(from the Peyton Jones family collection)

Achates : officers and ratings.

Killed : Lt Cdr.A.H.T.Johns ; Lt E.B.Marland ; S.Lt K.H.Highfield,RNR;
Surg.Lt J.L.B.MacFarlane ;
Missing : Lt (E) Peter Wright,RNR;
Died of wounds : S.Lt. F.R.Barrett,RNVR.

Survivors : S.Lt.A.J.Davidson; A/Gun (T) G.W.Smith; Chief Stoker
W.G.Brown ; S.P.O. T.G.Gogle; A/CP.O. D.Hall ; Yeoman A.W.Taylor

From awards :

Wright (Mention) for work with damage control ; Surg Lt James
MacFarlane (mention) was attending casualties on the bridge when
killed; Davies (DSC) courage and coolness when repairing electrical
leads etc; S.P.O. James Cole,working on plot until bridge hit,
then attended wounded and later helped to get them on to Carley
floats but was not rescued; A/B McIver,RNR, rescued wounded man
from flooded compartment,made several journeys along upper deck
under heavy fire,later took wheel steering by boat's compass,but
did not survive; P.O.Teleg William Bartrip,in charge of W/T until
put out of action,then tried to repair,later dealt with CBs and
reported the fact while in the water,but did not survive; Stoker
Joseph Colley,courage in engine room,later led community singing in
the water; A.B. Charles Brightmore,wounded in director but stayed
there until ordered to abandon;CPO Daniel Hall,at wheel when direct
hit on bridge,wounded but regained wheel; Yeoman Albert Taylor,
escaped when bridge hit,sent for senior surviving officer, sent
messages as ordered and was still doing so when ship sank; Teleg
Eric Dicnkenson,ordered to rig jury aerials while ship under fire,
knocked down by blast of bursting shell.

Northern Gem : Men who went over the side to rescue survivors
-Skipper John Pooley,A/Cox S.A.Kerslake,Engineman Edmonds,L/S
Douglas Parnell, Steward J.J.Fleming. O.S.(RDF) E.G.Mayer,aged
42,whose sister was a hospital nurse,nursed wounded in N.Gem.

Questions and answers between Dudley Pope, author of *73° North*,
and Loftus Peyton Jones (from the Peyton Jones family collection)

1. For approximately how long had Achates been making smoke before
the Hipper opened fire ? The RoP Close Escort says that at 0941 the
enemy opened fire at Achates "which by this time was very conspicuous
due to the smoke screen". Your report is not quite clear what time
you started making smoke.

2. Which salvo straddled, and which caused the near miss ~~straddle~~ on the
port side which holed the forward shell room, magazine and stokers'
messdeck, and caused splinters among the port Oerlikon and bridge
personnel ?

3. Which of the bridge personnel were wounded or killed by this ?

4. This damage was at about 0945 and at 1110 Achates was ordered to
"prolong the line to port". David Kinloch was told of the damage and
ordered Achates to the head of the convoy. The following question is
not being wise after the event, but I would like to put in the answer
to stop the question being asked by readers : had any attempt been
made to tell the SO before this that Achates had been damaged ?

5. Going back to before the action : while Obdurate was investigating
the destroyers, a tanker near the rear of the convoy was in some sort
of trouble, probably steering gear, and was burning rather bright
'Not under control' lights. This was engaging Onslow's attention when
the gun flashes were seen from the destroyers firing at Obdurate. Can
you remember anything about the tanker ?

6. Where were you when action stations was sounded ? What was you job
normally ? What was your action station - where, rather ?

7. When Hipper first opened fire, did Achates take avoiding action or
was there not time before the first near-miss ?

8. What was your job - or what did you do, rather - around the time
of the near miss ? I assume you were involved with damage control.

9. Can you outline the role of various other officers during this time ?
(With names) Same for any outstanding ratings. I have the recommendations
for awards for Lt Wright, Surg Lt Macfarlane, Davies, the Acting Gunner T,
and various others, including A/B McIver, who helped get men from
flooded compartments and later took the wheel for an hour, steering
only by a boat's compass; P.O. Teleg. Bartrip, who among other things
made sure all the CBs were locked in the safe and reported this
(presumably to you)while in the water; Steward Allan Jones, who
stayed with the wounded on board when the ship sank ; Stoker
Colley, who led community singing while in the water waiting to be
picked up; CPO Hall, at wheel when the ship was hit on the bridge,
and the only survivor in the wheelhouse ; the Yeoman, Taylor, one of the
few survivors from the bridge hit, who sent for you and who continued
passing signals etc, including the one interrupted by the ship capsizing.
    I have listed these as the more outstanding men : can you add
anything to the brief description of what they did ? Particularly
Taylor on handing over to you.

10. The hit on the bridge : where were you at this time, and what doing ? Who came and told you what had happened ? What did the bridge look like when you arrived ? The ship was circling under 20 degrees of wheel and doing 28 knots. *(I mention points like this in case they help your memory.)*

11. Can you remember the actual sequence of your actions from the time of coming on to the bridge ? Only the wheel and engine room telegraphs had escaped being wrecked. Your report says speed was reduced to 12 knots and smoke was ordered to be made, and Obedient's last order, for obvious reasons, was disregarded.

12. There were subsequent hits, but you continued making smoke, and using a boat's compass. This sounds a silly question, but has some relevance : do you remember which boat it came from, and could it be secured for the quartermaster it or was it held by hand ?

13. When Sheffield's signal arrived 'Report situation', did you assume it meant the situation in Achates or* for the whole convoy ? I see you say your signal reporting your own damage was cancelled before it was sent.

14. In your report there is a discrepancy in times, and I wonder if you can clear it up. A signal was sent to Northern Gem at 1300 'Not under control. Please stand by me' after the ship stopped and preparations were made for the ship to be taken in tow from aft. The list continued however until the upper deck was awash. A signal was then started to Northern Gem asking her to take you in tow, but was broken off as the ship rolled over. Then the report adds that Achates sunk at about 1300.

I want to establish the time sequence from the 'Not under control' signal. I wonder if you can outline what happened, with roughs times ?

I get the impression that to begin with, after the first signal, she was not listing very fast; but that from the time the signal was started to Northern Gem asking her to take you in tow, the final roll which put her on her beam ends, I imagine, must have been less than a couple of minutes.

15. Can you describe these last few moments in some detail ? Just how fast she went over, how the men got away from the ship, how quickly she sank, and how you yourself got away ?

16. In the water : can you describe this - how Northern Gem manoeuvred, how men were got aboard - I see from the awards that some of the N. Gem men went over the side themselves - the effect of the cold, incidents like Colley leading community singing, whether the swell was dispersing the groups of men, what percentage managed to get on to rafts etc.

I have been unable to get in touch with Aisthorpe - the only CO I've failed to find. So if you can describe events on Northern Gem after you got on board, it would be a great help.

17. The depth charges whose primers had frozen up went off 35 minutes after the ship sank. Do you suppose it took that time for them to thaw or was there any other possible reason ?

18. The awards mention Aisthorpe personally taking the wheel to bring

Northern Gem alongside Obdurate next day to get the doctor aboard. A moderate gale was blowing, so this was obviously no mean feat. Can you describe ?

19. Personal details about yourself, which, knowing you slightly, I know you'll hate giving ! But they are basic ones - were you a sub or lieutenant at the time ? How old were you ? How long had Johns been commanding Achates ? How long had you been in her ?

Loftus Peyton Jones' responses to Dudley Pope's Questions

H.M.S. "ACHATES".

BACKGROUND.

H.M.S. "ACHATES" recommissioned after a long refit at Swan Hunter's Yard on the Tyne in April, 1942. There she had been provided with a new bow, the original one having been virtually blown off by a mine when operating in Icelandic waters the previous year.

After the customary work up - brief but strenuous - she was assigned to the Clyde Special Escort Force, a force which had been formed as a small reserve of ships which could be used to reinforce the escort groups employed on the regular convoy cycles as occasion demanded.

And so it was from the friendly shores of Gourock that she was to operate for the final busy months of her career.

Her first real job was as part of the escort to P.Q. 16, the midsummer convoy to N. Russia which, under conditions of continuous daylight, suffered heavy and seemingly endless air attack throughout the last week of a brilliant May. Thus early in the new commission were the guns and their crews well tried.

A spell at Murmansk, an uneventful return convoy, a short period of boiler cleaning leave and "ACHATES" was off again to fulfil a similar function for P.Q. 18. This convoy, sailed in September, again suffered heavy air attack, though this time mainly from torpedo bombers. Together with U Boats they accounted for over a dozen ships. Most memorable from "ACHATES" point of view were the many abortive U Boat hunts in the very difficult Arctic conditions which prevail in those waters, and the fact that we opened our score against the Luftwaffe. Our destination this time was Archangel - remembered now only for its wooden construction and the number of nights on which we had to land parties of seamen to fight fires caused by incendiary bombs.

Then a rush back to the Clyde at a pleasant eighteen knots the whole way, a few days storing and on to Gib. to find the largest assembly of escorts we had ever seen. A week there of conferences and preparations and out to escort the great convoy of ships appearing magically from the Atlantic wastes and bound for the beaches of North Africa. Our role during a period of ten days or so involved only some desultory bombardment and a lot of patrolling off shore. When screening some heavy units on the passage back to Gib. we did, however, gain contact with a submarine and after several attacks were credited with having sunk her. Certainly there was much wreckage to be seen though I think she was probably of Vichy French origin.

Not so successful were our efforts on the homeward voyage when in a rising gale in the Bay of Biscay the empty troopship "WARWICK CASTLE" was torpedoed and sunk. It gave us, though, our first taste of the pitiful task of picking up survivors, the difficulties of getting

weakened/...

2.

weakened frightened men on to our slippery steel decks,
in resuscitating the apparently drowned, of burying the
dead and accommodating the living in our already over-
crowded mess decks.   However, all was in the end
accomplished and the end of November found us once more
alongside at Gourock snatching a few days leave wherever
our fancies lay.

Our Captain had changed after our
return from our first trip to N. Russia, A.A. Toit having
been replaced on his promotion to Commander by A.H.T. Johns.
A destroyer officer of the old school, he had started
us off in a tough unrelenting manner which made us learn
fast and think first and last of the efficiency of the
ship.   He was later to be lost in the Atlantic in H.M.S.
"HARVESTER".   More recently the Gunner (T) had been
replaced and we had gained an extra Sub Lieutenant
Davidson.   For this last trip we had a technical radar
officer on board whose name I have forgotten.   But
otherwise we were the same Wardroom that had recommissioned
the ship in April.

There was Eric Marland, brilliant graduate
of Magdalen College, Oxford, and now as a Lieutenant
R.N.V.R. with a D.S.C. and bar (the last awarded for the
sinking of our submarine in the Mediterranean) our No. 2.
Unperturbable, brave as only those with true faith can be,
completely competent and endowed with a modist assurance
and quiet cheerfulness that commanded the respect and
affection of us all.

There was Kenneth Highfield our Sub Lieutenant R.N.R., and inevitably, our Navigator, hardly
finished his apprenticeship with, I think, the P. & O.
but full of real enthusiasm for his job.   There was
Fred Barret, a cheerful young citizen of North London
with no knowledge of the sea but a determination to do
his damndest at any job entrusted to him.

And, of course, there was the Chief and
the Doctor.   The former, Peter Wright, another R.N.R.
Officer with more experience of hard seafaring than most
of us and a delightful twinkle in his eye as he led us
up the garden path.   The latter, James MacFarlane, doubt-
less an excellent doctor but more remembered by us as a
cheerful willing messmate prepared to turn his hand to
any of the hundred and one odd jobs that must be undertaken by some member of a destroyer Wardroom.

Of these only the Chief, the Radar Officer
and the new Gunner (T) Mr. Smith?, were married though
the Doctor had announced his engagement only a few
months before.

Of the Ships company I think the Coxswain
was the only senior rating to have changed and very
lucky we were to have A/C.P.O. Hall.

So/...

3.

So it was with a reasonably experienced ship's company that "ACHATES" set off for Seydisfiord in mid December from there to escort the Transatlantic ships which were to form part of Convoy J.W. 51B.

J.W. 51B.

With orders to sail from Seydisfiord on 24th December the burning question was whether or not to have our traditional Christmas dinner before we left or wait till our arrival the other end.   No compromise could be allowed to spoil our enjoyment of those excellent turkeys we had embarked at Gourock.   In the event it was decided to defer our gastronomic celebrations until arrival at Murmansk - a decision from which the moral is obvious.

The first six days of our passage passed much like any others of those spent on escorting convoys to North Russia, save only that the wind was more boisterous, the darkness more enveloping and the cold, perhaps, more severe.   After an early gale we spent much time chipping away the ice which clung to the superstructure, decks and guard rails and by increasing topweight made our rolling even more pronounced than it need have been.

But if we spent longer battling with the elements we were certainly less molested by the enemy and, apart from stragglers, had lost no ships from the convoy.

ACTION OF 31st DECEMBER.

Now to answer your specific questions.

1.   I would say we started making smoke at about 0930, i.e. some ten minutes before HIPPER opened fire. This would be ten minutes after going to action stations which again I think is about right.

2.   This is difficult for me to answer with any certainty but my impression was that the second and/or third salvo straddled and that the fourth or fifth salvos caused the near miss and first casualties on the port side.

3.   Two of the port oerlikon guns crew - just below the bridge - were wounded, one severely so.   One of the lookouts and, I think, a signalman were casualties on the bridge.   There were also about half a dozen casualties between decks-among the forward supply and fire and repair parties.

4.   I cannot say for certain but I do not think so, the reason probably being that it was only as time pro- gressed that the results of the damage i.e. the flooding of the lower messdecks, became apparent.   "ACHATES" had continued to fulfil her allotted task and it was, presumably, only when she was called upon to undertake a new one that it became imperative to inform the S.O. Escort of the damage sustained.

5/...

4.

5.   Regret No, although I heard mention of this incident later.

6.   I was just completing my tour of inspection of the Upper Deck, part of ship work having started at 0900, when I myself observed gun flashes astern.   By the time I arrived on the Bridge, the Captain was already there and "Action Stations" were being piped.   My own "Action Station" - nominally O.O.G. aft to be at the other end of the ship from the Captain - resolved itself on this occasion into a continuous tour of all quarters, locating and inspecting damage, co-ordinating damage control measures, replacing casualties and generally seeing that all hands were best employed, keeping the Bridge informed, etc.

7.   Again I cannot say for certain, not having been on the Bridge at that moment but I would have thought so although there would not have been much time for any evasive action taken to have much effect.

8.   See answer to 6 above.

9.   I have enlarged on the activities of some of those you mention in answering other questions.   For the remainder, I fear, the recommendation for awards will have to suffice, since any further comment by me at this stage would probably be inaccurate.

As you will realise the selection of those you quote for awards was only made after hearing accounts of their conduct from other survivors and I did not necessarily observe all their actions personally.

10.   In the T.S., having heard, whilst engaged with the For'd D.C. Parties, that the enemy was again in sight.

That the ship had been hit was unmistakable; the noise of the explosion and the shock to the ship was appreciable even in the T.S.   A quick check for'd and aft at the level of the upper deck - the deck on which the T.S. was situated - revealed nothing new so I started up to the Bridge.   At the foot of the first ladder I was met by a white faced youngster sent by the Yeoman to fetch me. Arrival in the wheelhouse it became obvious that the hit had been on the Bridge.   The deckhead was bulging downward and a somewhat dazed Coxswain was ruefully regarding the wreckage around him.

The usual way up to the Bridge was barred, so stepping out on to the port Oerlikon gun platform I clambered up the remains of the outside ladder.   The familiar scene was unrecognisable - just a blackened shambles of twisted metal with the remains of a few identifiable objects sticking grotesquely out of the wreckage.   Among this fantastic jumble of what had been the Compass Platform lay the mercifully unidentifiable remains of those whose station had been on this fore part of the Bridge.   Captain, No. 2 and Navigator, Signalmen, A/S Operators and maybe others.   Over all hung the stench of acrid fumes and burnt flesh.

Further aft the damage was less severe although still effectively flattened as if by some giant hammer smashing down from above. There were bodies lying and not

all/...

5.

all of them dead.   I leant over Fred Barrett who had been
directing the gun armament, but he was too badly wounded to
tell me anything.   And then I saw the Yeoman who by some
miracle had survived where all others had been struck down.
He was leaning against the jagged after screen, dazed but
apparently unhurt as he straightened up and smiled on seeing
me.   Slowly - muddlingly so to start with but becoming
more coherent as his full senses returned - he told me of
the state of the battle as he knew it.

11.   There was much to be done.   First to
establish communication with the wheelhouse below - through
a hole in the deck - and to hear the reassuring voice of
the Coxswain answering in response to my order, that the
wheel was now amidships.   Then to start an erratic zig
zag whilst endeavouring to get word to the guns (B and Y
mountings) of the bearing of the enemy, for we were still
under fire though apart from his gun flashes it was difficult
to see our opponent.

                        B Gun crew had, however, largely been put
out of action by the shell exploding on the front of the
bridge and though replacements were conscripted by Sub Lt.
Davidson - whose cheerful face appeared from nowhere - the
mounting was found to be jammed in training.   And Y Gun
apparently never received the order leaving one to conclude
that the messenger was killed on his way aft.

                        Meanwhile the ominous glow on B Gun Deck -
a cordite fire apparently started by the explosion on the
bridge and had, I was relieved to note, been extinguished.
As much, I learnt later, by the spray as by the efforts of
the relief crew but anyway it was one anxiety out of the
way.

                        It was not long - perhaps five minutes or
even less - before the firing ceased and the enemy was lost
to view.   Speed was at once reduced to relieve the strain
on the damaged hull and to give us time to sort ourselves
out.

                        Of the tactical situation I knew only what
little I had gleaned from my occasional visits to the
Bridge to report the progress of affairs between decks,
and the present situation was certainly somewhat obscure.
Certainly the convoy was still there with its close
corvette and trawler escort, but the present movements and
future intentions of the remaining destroyers were as
unknown as the composition and likely action of the enemy.

                        From the Yeoman's report of the exchange
of signals with "OBEDIENT" it was apparent that she had
now taken over as Senior Officer in place of the presumably damaged "ONSLOW" who had been sent to the disengaged
side of the enemy.   It was equally apparent that we
were in no state to take anyone under our orders and until
we had our own situation under control it seemed best to
stay where we were and make the only effective contribution
to the defence of the convoy of which we were capable -
namely laying smoke.   Orders were accordingly passed by
word of mouth to the Engine Room to recommence making smoke
and as the black clouds started rolling out of the funnel
the ship was conned on a broad weave across the stern of
the convoy.

                                        Steering/...

6.

Steering became difficult with the increasing
list to port and a trim by the head and our progress would
have been even more erratic without the aid of a boat's
compass.   This was fetched from one of the sea boats,
on whose orders - mine or the coxswains - I can not now
remember, and wedged in the wrecked fore bulkhead of the
wheelhouse.   The bearings it portrayed were obviously
inaccurate but it was adequate for the purpose.

It was about this time that Chief's head appeared
over the side of the Bridge to report the situation below.
It was not rosy.   Further damage had been sustained
during those last minutes the ship was under fire, which
had resulted in the flooding of No. 2 Boiler Room and of
a further section of lower deck compartments.   There had
also been more casualties including, it appeared, the
Doctor, for he could nowhere be found.

12.   See answer to No. 11 above.

13.   As reported verbally from the W/T Office at the
time I took this signal from "SHEFFIELD" to have been
addressed to "ACHATES".   In retrospect I imagine it must
have been addressed to the S.O. Escort.   My reply was,
I am virtually certain, sent by light to "NORTHERN GEM" but
cancelled before she had time to transmit it in view of the
rapidly worsening situation.

14.   The time of sinking should, I think, read 1330,
though naturally all times are pretty approximate,
certainly there was an appreciable interval between the
time of being forced to stop and the time the ship sank -
I would say about half an hour.

"NORTHERN GEM" did not immediately respond to
our first signal asking her to standby and it was only when
we were seen to be capsizing that she cracked on speed and
arrived literally in the nick of time.   Her skipper later
explained that the first message was so badly transmitted
(by light) - as well it might have been under the circumstances - that he half suspected it to have been made by
the enemy as some sort of ruse de guerre.   He, therefore,
approached somewhat circumspectly.

As far as we were concerned there would have
been no survivors if that message - made by the Yeoman on
a box lamp salvaged from the flag deck - had not been
received and acted upon.

15.   Time on the Bridge between about 1200 and 1300
passed slowly.   The Chief and Sub. Lt. Davidson looked
up occasionally to make brief reports of progress, the
former on the losing battle to control the flooding in the
ship and the latter on the measures being taken to collect
and care for the casualties of which by now there were a
considerable number.

Shells bursting on impact with the water just
short of the ship had riddled the port side with holes and
wounded many men.   There was plenty for the remainder to
do and hands were fallen out from Action Stations and
marshalled into repair parties under the direction of the
Engineer Officer in a vain effort to save the ship.

But/...

7.

But on the Bridge there was little to do but
wait and think ...   The course of the battle was
difficult to make out although it appeared that attack on
the convoy had been beaten off for the time being.   The
whereabouts of the enemy were unknown.   Doubts of the
effectiveness of our smoke screen were relieved by the
exchange of signals with "HYDERABAD".   Meanwhile it was
getting dark and cold.

Eventually there was Chief's report of the
impossibility of maintaining steam and our resulting signal
to "NORTHERN GEM".   The Sub. was ordered, as a precaution,
to clear away boats and rafts and then to prepare the
ship to be taken in tow aft.   He said it would be
difficult getting any cable aft so I told him not to worry
about that.   I must admit that I had grown so used to
the list to port that I had not realised just how bad it
was.   But when I eventually moved to the after end of the
Bridge and saw the whaler, still at the davit head, awash,
it was brought home to me just how great the odds were
against remaining afloat.

A final word to Chief and everyone was
ordered on the upper deck though preparations for being
taken in tow were to continue.   The last signal to "NORTHERN
GEM" was started but the list quite suddenly started to
increase rapidly and I told the Yeoman to desist.   Within
a couple of minutes the ship was on her beam ends and the
Yeoman and I scrambled on to the now horizontal starboard
side of the wheelhouse.   The door at our feet was open and
we hoisted a couple of men out of the murky shambles below -
one of whom was, I think, the wounded Fred Barrett.   I
just had time to unsling my binoculars from round my neck
and to hang them on a convenient projection when the water
surged around us.

16.   In the turmoil of the next few minutes I lost
touch with my late companions on the side of the Bridge,
but remember noting with satisfaction the number of carley
floats and rafts that had floated off and mentally
congratulating the Sub Lieutenant on his work.   One empty
carley float was only some twenty five yards off and to
this I swam and climbed on to it.   My principal concern
now was that "NORTHERN GEM" might not see us in the gathering
darkness and so for several minutes I held aloft the special
light with which these floats were then provided, thanking
Providence that it was functioning correctly.

Calling to various heads in the water congre-
gated some fifteen or twenty men round the float, among
them the Coxswain and P.O. Tel., both apparently as
unruffled as ever.   Some were supporting their wounded
shipmates and these we man handled on to the raft.   I told
them "NORTHERN GEM" was on the way to pick us up and we
started singing "Roll out the Barrel"......

It was not long before the Trawler appeared
circling the spot where "ACHATES" had gone down and as she
stopped in the middle of the group of bobbing rafts we

paddled/...

8.

paddled ourselves towards her.   Someone threw us a line
and this I made fast round the carley float.   As we
drew alongside, however, everyone crowded to one side and
the raft capsized.   Willing hands stretched down to
haul us out of the water but what with the swell and the
height of the trawler's bulwarks it was no easy matter and
we had to wait with what patience we could muster.   Many
had not the strength to hold the ropes that were thrown
them and the crew of "NORTHERN GEM" climbed out on to the
rubbing strake to heave them inboard.   Even so it seemed
to take a long time and while waiting I climbed back on to
the carley raft, and took off my sheepskin coat and sea-
boots.   One lone swimmer appeared alongside and him I
hauled on to the float.   We were eventually among the
last to get on board from that side by which time arms and
legs were pretty numb, and instinct had replaced cohesive
thought.

Meanwhile other groups clinging to floats
and rafts had paddled up to "NORTHERN GEM" and been hauled
on board.   Among them was the group whose singing was so
strongly being led by Colley -   As the Mate of the Trawler
afterwards remarked "He deserved a medal as big as a plate".

From the deck of "NORTHERN GEM" I looked
round for a moment for any last sign of "ACHATES" - but
there was nothing.   I learnt afterwards that she rolled
right over and hanging a few seconds with her rudder and
propellers in the air, slid quickly out of sight.

Hustled below I found myself in the warm and
well lit foc'sle surrounded by the majority of my fellow
survivors, and the somewhat emotional scenes of the next
half hour are better not described.   Suffice to say that
"NORTHERN GEM" being specially fitted for the rescue of
survivors there were bunks, blankets and dry kits for everyone and her crew, though heavily outnumbered, worked
tirelessly on our behalf.

After a couple of hours, by which time I
felt well restored, I was sought out by the Mate and
conducted aft to the WardRoom - with many apologies for not
earlier having realised that I was on board!   Here I
found the Sub. Lieut. - Davidson and the Gunner - Smith,
both equally surprised to see me, and heard their accounts
of their experiences.   Then for the first time I went up
to the Bridge to meet Skipper Aisethorpe and to thank him
for his ready assistance.   I was impressed with his
competence and real humanity and learnt that this was not
the first time on which he had been called upon to rescue
sailors from the sea.

He was still out of touch with the convoy and
we discussed the best course to steer.   Later that evening
"OBEDIENT" overhauled us from astern and over the loud
hailer I told David Kinloch of the loss of "ACHATES".
I think this was the first he knew of it.   Anyway he
confirmed our course and by the following morning the
convoy was again in sight.   Incidentally there were many
anxious minutes on board as a ship was detected closing
from astern and before she was identified as "OBEDIENT".

Meanwhile/...

9.

Meanwhile the Coxswain had prepared a list of all survivors on board and everything possible was done for the wounded. The worst of them was Fred Barrett who had miraculously made his way across, but now stood in urgent need of medical attention; but in the absence of a doctor there was little enough we could do.

17.   I really do not know.   I only found out later that several primers had been so iced up to be immovable, and so had been left in the charges.   Presumably the pistols were iced up too and it was the time taken for them to function that occasioned the delay since the primers would very quickly have been forced into their firing position by the pressure of water.

In "NORTHERN GEM" we all felt the explosion but I did not connect it with "ACHATES" depth charges until Skipper Aisethorpe suggested it to me.   I was glad that he added that by that time there were no more survivors in sight – not that I think anyone would have survived more than half an hour in that water.

18.   The last evening of 1942 was for us memorable only for the shock we felt at the loss of so many of our shipmates and our anxiety for the lives of those who seemed unlikely to survive.   The grey dawn of New Years Day was equally cheerless though once again in touch with the convoy it did at least promise the services of a doctor.

The wind had increased during the night and by the time we were ordered alongside "OBDURATE" to receive her Medical Officer it was blowing a moderate gale. "OBDURATE" reduced speed and ceased zig zagging but even so was yawing considerably.   "NORTHERN GEM" too was being thrown about by the sea and it was in these circumstances as the trawler closed the destroyers port quarter, that Skipper Aisethorpe took the wheel.   With watchful care and great patience, evidently borne of long experience, he edged "NORTHERN GEM" closer and closer until only twenty feet separated the two ships.   Fenders were provided by both vessels but the manoevre looked likely to be hazardous in the extreme.   Then, judging the moment perfectly, Aisethorpe put his bow right alongside "OBDURATE's" Q.D. and with commendable promptitude the doctor jumped the six vertical feet which separated the level of the two decks.   His bag was thrown after him and the ships sheered away from each other with no worse damage than a little scratched paint.

To effect this transfer in the conditions then prevailing was no easy matter and virtually the whole credit for its successful execution must go to Skipper Aisethorpe. His display of seamanship was of a very high order.

We were more than glad to see the doctor – a young Surgeon Lieutenant R.N.V.R. named Hood, who was subsequently himself to lose his life at sea – though quite under what circumstances I do not know.   He certainly laboured hard that day and must have saved several lives.

Under most difficult conditions, both of hygiene and equilibrium, he calmly went from patient to patient,
cleaning/...

10.

cleaning, cutting, stitching and bandaging till all were
attended to.   I, myself, accompanied him throughout and
learnt a lot in the process – even to the extent of
administering anaesthetics to those on whom he had
to operate.   It was evening before we had finished.
Only for Fred Barrett had he been unable to do very much
and this officer died uncomplainingly that night.

        The prayer book which Skipper Aisethorpe
handed me the next morning had the burial service well
marked from previous occasions. . Permission was obtained
from "OBEDIENT" to stop the ship for a few minutes and
a brief but poignant Service was held attended by all
the survivors and the crew of "NORTHERN GEM".

        It was not the first time I had had to read
these prayers but on this occasion there was that added
depth of feeling as we said a symbolic farewell to so
many of our shipmates.

19.   Lieutenant.   24.   See "Background".

———————

Transcription from the BBC about the loss of the *Achates*

"The Board of Admiralty regrets to announce that His Majesty's destroyer ACHATES (Lieutenant-Commander A.H. Tyndall Johns, R.N.) was damaged in the defence of the convoy and subsequently sank. H.M.S. ONSLOW suffered some damage and casualties. The next-of-kin of the casualties in both these ships have been informed."

ACHATES, which had a displacement of thirteen-hundred-and-thirty tons, was completed in 1930 and carried four 4.7-inch guns. She was adopted by the town of Halesowen, in Worcestershire. H.M.S. ONSLOW, another Warship Week destroyer, was adopted by Oldham. Both vessels were built by Messrs. John Brown and Company at Clydebank, the ONSLOW was completed since the outbreak of the

6

war. Captain Sherbrooke was previously with H.M.S. COSSACK, and gained the D.S.O. in June 1940 for the part he played in the second battle of Narvik.

B.B.C   NEWS   REPORT   OF   SINKING.

Appendix 3

Fred Bean naval service photographs

Fred Bean

Fred Bean and friends in Iceland

Appendix 4

David Macdonald family papers

BUCKINGHAM PALACE

The Queen and I offer you
our heartfelt sympathy in your
great sorrow.

We pray that your country's
gratitude for a life so nobly
given in its service may bring
you some measure of consolation.

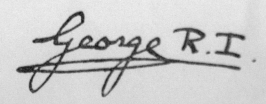

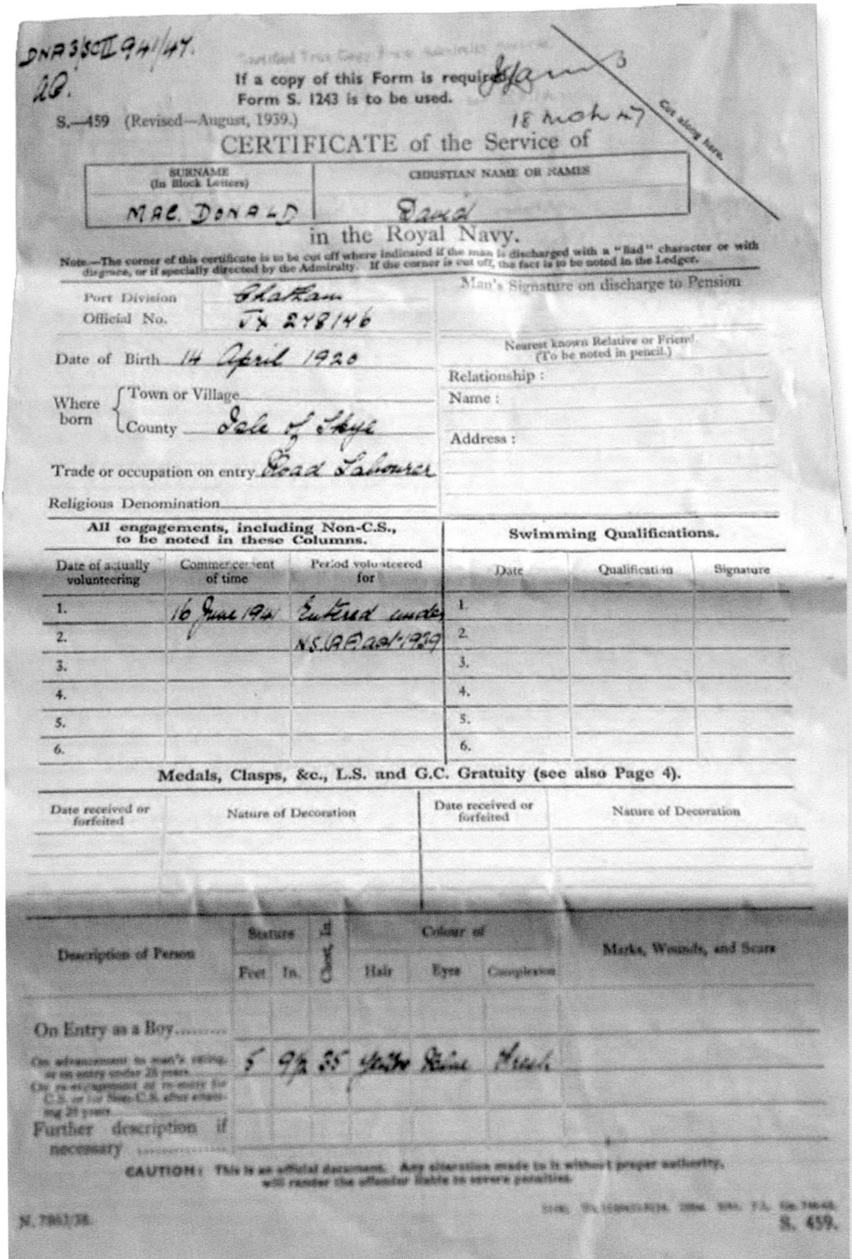

DNA3/SCII 941/47.
AB.

If a copy of this Form is required Form S. 1243 is to be used.

S.—459 (Revised—August, 1939.) 18 Mch 47

Cut along here.

CERTIFICATE of the Service of

SURNAME (In Block Letters)	CHRISTIAN NAME OR NAMES
MAC. DONALD	David

in the Royal Navy.

Note.—The corner of this certificate is to be cut off where indicated if the man is discharged with a "Bad" character or with disgrace, or if specially directed by the Admiralty. If the corner is cut off, the fact is to be noted in the Ledger.

Port Division Chatham
Official No. JX 278146

Man's Signature on discharge to Pension

Date of Birth 14 April 1920

Nearest known Relative or Friend (To be noted in pencil.)
Relationship :
Name :
Address :

Where born: Town or Village
County Isle of Skye

Trade or occupation on entry Road Labourer

Religious Denomination

All engagements, including Non-C.S., to be noted in these Columns.

Date of actually volunteering	Commencement of time	Period volunteered for
1.	16 June 1941	Entered under
2.		N.S.(A)Act 1939
3.		
4.		
5.		
6.		

Swimming Qualifications.

	Date	Qualification	Signature
1.			
2.			
3.			
4.			
5.			
6.			

Medals, Clasps, &c., L.S. and G.C. Gratuity (see also Page 4).

Date received or forfeited	Nature of Decoration	Date received or forfeited	Nature of Decoration

Description of Person	Stature Feet	Stature In.	Chest	Colour of Hair	Colour of Eyes	Colour of Complexion	Marks, Wounds, and Scars
On Entry as a Boy							
On advancement to man's rating, or on entry under 18 years	5	9½	35	Yellow	Blue	Fresh	
On re-engagement or re-entry for C.S. or for Non-C.S. after attaining 28 years							
Further description if necessary							

CAUTION: This is an official document. Any alteration made to it without proper authority, will render the offender liable to severe penalties.

N. 7863/38. S. 459.

David Macdonald's service papers

David Macdonald's service papers

David Macdonald as a boy in Waternish

David with his mother and father and his sister at home in Lusta, Waternish

David with parents and siblings at home in Lusta, Waternish

Appendix 5

Items relating to Kenneth MacIver from his son John MacIver

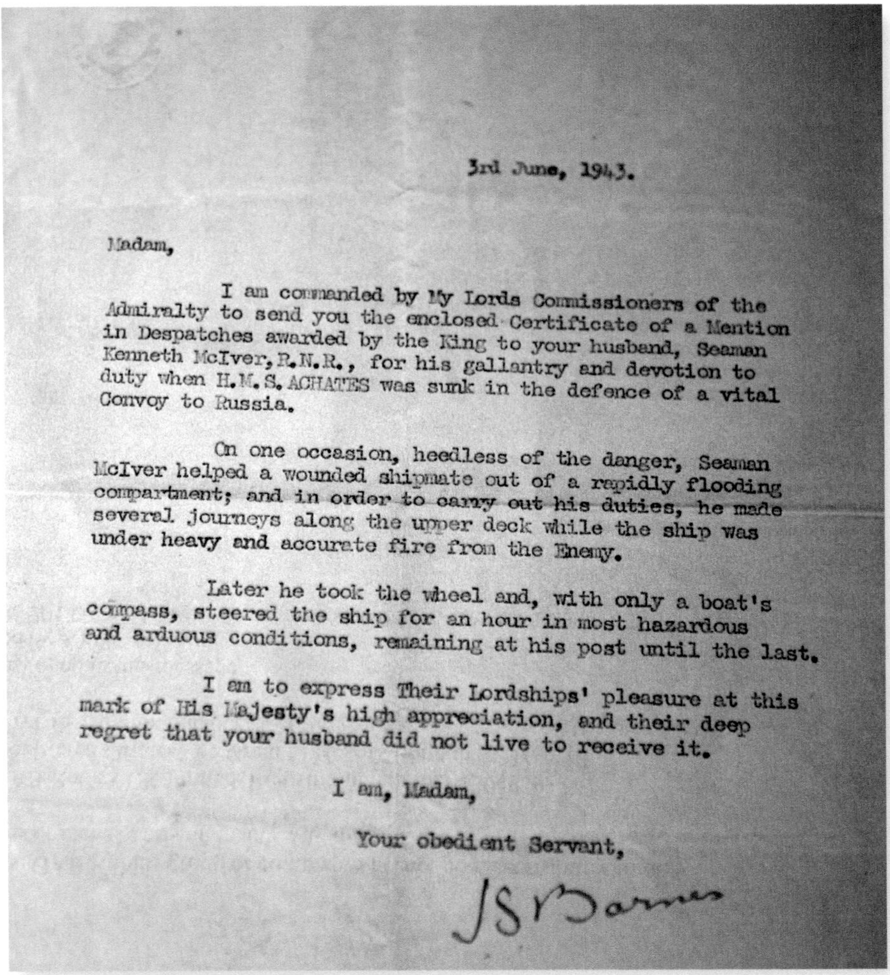

3rd June, 1943.

Madam,

I am commanded by My Lords Commissioners of the Admiralty to send you the enclosed Certificate of a Mention in Despatches awarded by the King to your husband, Seaman Kenneth McIver, R.N.R., for his gallantry and devotion to duty when H.M.S. ACHATES was sunk in the defence of a vital Convoy to Russia.

On one occasion, heedless of the danger, Seaman McIver helped a wounded shipmate out of a rapidly flooding compartment; and in order to carry out his duties, he made several journeys along the upper deck while the ship was under heavy and accurate fire from the Enemy.

Later he took the wheel and, with only a boat's compass, steered the ship for an hour in most hazardous and arduous conditions, remaining at his post until the last.

I am to express Their Lordships' pleasure at this mark of His Majesty's high appreciation, and their deep regret that your husband did not live to receive it.

I am, Madam,

Your obedient Servant,

JSRBarnes

Letter informing Kenneth MacIver's widow that he was to be honoured

Kenneth MacIver's medal with 'Oak Leaf'

By the KING'S Order the name of
Seaman Kenneth McIver, R.N.R,
H.M.S.Achates,
was published in the London Gazette on
27 April, 1943,
as mentioned in a Despatch for distinguished service.
I am charged to record
His Majesty's high appreciation.

First Lord of the Admiralty

Notice of Kenneth MacIver's death from the government

Kenneth MacIver at home in Lewis
in his naval uniform

NESS

On Leave.—The following men and women of H.M. Forces were home on leave last week:—Donald Macleod, R.N.R., Eoropie, Port-of-Ness; Donald Macleod, R.N.R., do.; Norman Murray, R.N.R., do; P.O. Angus Mackay, R.N.R., Fivepenny; Norman Morrison, R.N.R., 35 Lionel; John Maclean, R.N.R., 118 Cross Skigersta Road; Finlay Murray, S.P., R.A.F., Back Street, Habost, Ness; Donald Macleod R.N.R., 119 Cross-Skigersta Road; Doleen Smith, N.A.A.F.I., Lionel, Port-of-Ness; Mary Ferguson, N.A.A. F.I., Manageress, Eoropie, Ness.

Lost on Active Service.—The whole township of Habost was cast into gloom when it became known that P.O. Kenny Maciver, R.N.R., husband of Doleen Murray, Back Street, Habost, Ness, has been lost at sea. Kenny Maciver belonged to North Tolsta, but married a Habost bride since war began, and made so many friends in the village that he might have belonged to it all his life. Kenny was on dangerous service all the time, and made several voyages to Russia with convoys, a trying job in the winter months. He was well liked by all who knew him and we in Habost will always remember his happy smile and cheery ways. He leaves a wife and one child at Ness. His sister, Mrs Donald Morrison, also resides in Ness, at 2 Habost. We deeply sympathise with them in their great loss.

NORTH TOLSTA

Killed in Action.—The price of peace is rising steadily. Once again it is our sad duty to report the death of one of our lads. Kenneth Maciver, R.N.R., 35 North Tolsta, has been killed in action at sea. He was on a destroyer. Kenny was at one time a piper in the Seaforth Highlanders, but had joined the R.N.R. before the war. He was at home about a month ago. To his young widow and son, at Habost, Ness, and his aged parents here, we extend our sympathy.

On Leave.—On leave this week are Donald and James Macdonald, R.N.R., 6 New Tolsta; George Morrison, 4 New Tolsta; Allan Murray, 49 North Tolsta; Murdo Macdonald, 38 North Tolsta; Alexander Nicholson, 9 Shore Street, all R.N.R.'s. Kenneth Macmillan, Glen Tolsta, has joined up and has left for a naval depot. Mary Ann Morrison, 4 New Tolsta, who recently completed her training as an orthopaedic nurse, has been appointed a sister at the Victoria Infirmary, Glasgow.

Notice of Kenneth MacIver's death in
the Stornoway Gazette

Appendix 6

Loch Ewe as Royal Navy Base

Isle of Ewe and Royal Navy base

Crane on pier, Loch Ewe

Nissen huts Loch Ewe

Aerial shot of Loch Ewe and Royal Navy base

Bibliography and Sources

Books

Hague, Arnold. *Convoy Rescue Ships*. Gravesend. World Ship Society, 1998

Hague, Arnold. *The Allied Convoy System, 1939-1945: Its Organization, Defence and Operation*. London. Greenhill Books, 2000

Hilar, A.P. *Sonar: Detector of Submerged Submarines*. Navy Department Office of the Chief of Naval Operation. Washington D.C. 1946, Accessed in Google Books

Llewllyn Jones, M. *The Royal Navy and Arctic Convoys: A Naval Staff History. Routledge*, 2007 Accessed in Google Books

Mellhuish, Arnold. *Commodore Robin Aveline Mellhuish*. Gairloch. Wordworks, 2013

Pearson, Michael. *Red Sky in the Morning*. Barnsley. Pen and Sword Maritime, 2007

Peyton Jones, Loftus. *Wartime Wanderings 1939–45*. Edited edition by JC Peyton Jones. Create Space Independent Publishing Platform, 2019

Pope, Dudley. *73° North, The Battle of the Barents Sea*. London. Weidenfeld and Nicolson, 1958

Shirer, William L. *The Rise and Fall of the Third Reich*. London. Book Club Associates by arrangement with Sucker and Wartburg Ltd., 1972

Walling, Michael G., e-book, *Forgotten Sacrifice, The Arctic Convoys of World War II*, Osprey Publishing, 2012

Wood, Mr and Mrs D. *Fidus Achates*. South Shields. Self-published, 2002

Woodman, R. *Arctic Convoys*. London. John Murray Press, 1994

Websites

BBC WW2 People's War. http://www.bbc.co.uk/history/ ww2peopleswar/ https://www.german-navy.de/kriegsmarine/articles/feature5.html

Kerslake, SA. "Coxswain in the Northern Convoys". www. naval-history. net/WW2Memoir-RussianConvoyCoxswain04.htm

Mackay, R. in "Britain's Fleet Air Arm in World War Two" in https:// en.wikipedia.org/wiki/Operation_EF_(1941)#cite_note-footnoteMackay2005141,_140-19 Rear-Admiral Mason in "*The Defence of Convoy JW51B.*" www.worldnavalships.com/forums

Weyman, Ronald. "Minefield: The Mining of HMS Achates, 25 July 1941." *Canadian Military History: Vol. 9: Iss. 2, Article 9* (2000) Available at: http://scholars.wlu.ca/cmh/vol9/iss2/9

Private Collections

David Macdonald's Family papers and photographs supplied by Allan R Macdonald (nephew) and Davina Matthews (niece).

Kenneth MacIver's Family Papers and photographs supplied by his son, John MacIver.

Andrew MacIver, Radar Operator, HMS *Sheffield*. Information supplied by his son, Andrew MacIver.

Papers and photographs pertaining to Loftus Peyton Jones. Supplied by his son, James Peyton Jones.

Personal account of Sinking of HMS *Achates* and photographs by Fred Bean. Supplied by his sons, David and Jim Bean.

Lectures

Arnold Melhuish, Convoy Commodores. Loch Ewe *Russian Convoy Conference*. May 2013

Captain Richard Woodman FRHistS FNI – author of *The Arctic Convoys 1941–45 and History of the British Merchant Navy* – Script delivered by Nick Hewitt on account of Captain Woodman being indisposed at Loch Ewe *Russian Convoy Conference*. May 2013

Jak Mallmann Showell. *U–Boats, German Navy, Torpedo Bombers and Enigma*. Loch Ewe Russian Convoy Conference. May 2013

Surgeon Commander GH Grant McMillan MD FRCP FRCP (Glasgow) Naval Medical Historian: Lecture on *Care of the Sick*

Endnotes

Chapter 1

1. https://winstonchurchill.org/resources/speeches/1940-the-finest-hour/ their-finest-hour/

2. https://www.britannica.com/place/Germany/World-War-II (Paragraph 4)

3. Mackay R, in Britain's Fleet Air Arm in World War Two quoted in https://en.wikipedia.org/wiki/Operation_EF_(1941)#cite_note-FOOTNOTE Mackay 2005141, 140-19

4. https://www.bbc.co.uk/history/ww2peopleswar/stories/38/a1090838.shtml Steve Adams story

5. Weyman, Ronald (2000) "*Minefield: The Mining of HMS Achates, 25 July 1941,*" Canadian Military History: Vol. 9: Iss. 2, Article 9. available at: http://scholars.wlu.ca/cmh/vol9/iss2/9

Chapter 2

6. http://www.bbc.co.uk/history/ww2peopleswar/stories/25/a8796225.shtml

7. https://www.bbc.co.uk/history/ww2peopleswar/stories/38/a1090838.shtml

8. The expression 'The Articles of War' was first used in 1637 in a book written by General Robert Monro: *Monro, His expedition with the worthy Scots regiment called Mac-keyes regiment.*

9. www.bbc.co.uk/history/ww2peopleswar/stories/38/a1090838.shtml

Chapter 3

10. https://www.bbc.co.uk/history/, ww2peopleswar/stories/75/a8249475.shtml

11. Werth, Alexander, p30 https://ia601504.us.archive.org/24/items/in.ernet.dli.2015.53301/2015.53301.Year-Of-Stalingrad-An-HistoricalRecord-And-A-Study-Of-Rissian-Mentality-Methods-And-Policies_text.pdf

12. http://www.theracmproject.org/roy-dykes.php and https://www.telegraph.co.uk/history/world-war-two/9895036/At-last-the- Arctic-Starfor-the-cold-war-warriors.html

Chapter 4

13. https://uboat.net/ops/convoys/convoys.php?convoy=PQ-16 for information and picture of *Syros* and https://www.wrecksite.eu/wreck. aspx?58245

14. See Woodman, R, *Artic Convoys*, p. 150 and also *The Royal Navy and the Arctic Convoys: A Naval Staff History*, edited by Malcolm Llewellyn-Jones

15. *Sonar: Detector of Submerged Submarines*, AP Hilar, Page 8

16. https://maritime.org/doc/uboat/index.htm#par250

17. Information from talk by Jak Showell at Loch Ewe, May 2013.

18. Information from talk by Jak Showell at Loch Ewe, May 2013.

Chapter 5

19. https://www.youtube.com/watch?v=VrspyzYUTNs&t=186s and http://www.russianarcticconvoymuseum.org/home/dykes-roy

20. *The Royal Navy and Arctic Convoys: A Naval Staff History*, M Llewllyn Jones, Chapter 3.

Chapter 6

21. https://www.bbc.co.uk/history/ww2peopleswar/stories/15/a2223415.shtml (Accessed 2022)

22. Written by Malcolm Macleod, Carloway, Isle of Lewis, who served on an escort minesweeper on the Russian Convoys. Courtesy of *Stornoway Gazette*.

Chapter 7

23. See https://www.history.navy.mil/ browse-by-topic/wars-conflicts-and-operations/world-war-ii/1942/atlantic/ pq-17.html for photographs of PQ17 under attack (Accessed 2022)

Chapter 8

24. Melhuish, pp3-4

25. Melhuish, p21

26. *Sacrifice for Stalin: The Sacrifice to Keep the Soviets in the Second World War* by David Wragg. Appendix II

27. Arnold Melhuish, *Convoy Commodores*. Lecture at Loch Ewe *Russian Convoy Conference*. May 2013

28. Melhuish, p53

Chapter 9

29. Convoy Rescue Ships, p9

30. See also http://historicalrfa.org/archived-stories68/1116-convoy-rescue-ships-service – James R Smith (Accessed 2022)

31. https://www.bbc.co.uk/history/ww2peopleswar/stories/90/a4048490.shtml - brenshaw

32. *Convoy Rescue Ships*, Hague, p21

33. *Convoy Rescue Ships*, Hague, p13

34. Lecture, Friday 10 May 2013 at Loch Ewe given by Surgeon Commander GH Grant McMillan MD FRCP FRCP (Glasgow) Naval Medical Historian

35. *Convoy Rescue Ships*, p14

36. Anatoli Lifshits, Russian War Veteran quoted in https://www.rbth.com/longreads/arctic_convoys/

37. Coxswain in the Northern Convoys by S A Kerslake, Chapter 4 – CONVOY PQ.17, *The Russian convoy "massacre" June 1942* https://www.naval-history. net/WW2 Memoir-RussianConvoyCoxswain04.htm

38. Kerslake, Chapter 4 – Convoy PQ.17

39. McMillan, Loch Ewe talk 2013

40. McMillan, Loch Ewe talk 2013

41. McMillan, Loch Ewe talk 2013

42. Hague, Convoy Rescue Ships, pp44-45

43. McMillan, Loch Ewe talk 2013

44. https://en.wikipedia.org/wiki/Robert_Dougall

Chapter 10

45. *The Rise and Fall of the Third Reich*, Shirer, p673

46. *The Rise and Fall of the Third Reich*, Shirer, p674

Chapter 11

47. Peyton Jones family papers held at https://digital.library.villanova.edu/Item/

48. Letter from Jack Fincham in Peyton Jones Family Collection held at Digital Library@Villanova University

Chapter 12

49. http://indicatorloops.com/lochewe.htm

Chapter 13

50. *Wartime Wanderings*, p117

51. *Red Sky in the Morning*, p36

Chapter 14

52. https://www.marxists.org/reference/archive/stalin/works/correspondence/02/41.htm%20 No.8

53. *The Hinge of Fate*, Churchill Winston S, p240

54. *73° North*, p60

55. Melhuish, p39

Chapter 16

56. *Red Sky in the Morning*, p37

Chapter 17

57. *Wartime Wanderings*, p119-120

58. *Wartime Wanderings*, p120

Chapter 18

59. *73° North*, p134

Chapter 19

60. *73° North*, p134

61. *73° North*, p138 – the actual message said PQ20. This was technically correct, but the allies had changed the convoy numbering systems, but the Germans had not captured the new code.

62. *73° North*, p140

Chapter 20

63. *73° North*, p143

64. *73° North*, p143

65. *Red Sky in the Morning*, p54

66. *Red Sky in the Morning*, p55

67. *Red Sky in the Morning*, p56

68. *Red Sky in the Morning*, p56

Chapter 21

69. *73° North*, pp126-128

70. *73° North*, p127

71. *73° North*, p128 and D Wood, Fidus Achates, unpublished paper, pp29-30

Chapter 22

72. *Wartime Wanderings*, pp121-122

Chapter 23

73. *Red Sky in the Morning*, p57

74. *73° North*, p179

75. *Wartime Wanderings, p122*

76. *Wartime Wanderings*, p122

77. *Wartime Wanderings*, p122

Chapter 24

78. *73° North, p181*

79. *73° North*, p181

80. *73° North*, p181-182

81. *Red Sky in the Morning*, p60

82. *73° North*, p189

83. *73° North*, p192

Chapter 25

84. *73° North*, p192

85. *Red Sky in the Morning*, p67

86. *73° North*, pp 204-205

Chapter 26

87. *An Account of The Battle of the Barents Sea*, 31/12/1942 in Frederick Bean's private papers, The Bean Family

88. Personal interview with David Bean by telephone, and in person in London

89. Peyton Jones family papers held at https://digital.library.villanova.edu/Item/vudl:41472

90. *Wartime Wanderings*, p124

91. *Wartime Wanderings*, pp125-126'

92. *Wartime Wanderings*, p126

93. *Arctic Convoys,* Woodman, p322

Chapter 27

94. *73° North*, p213

95. *73° North*, p213

96. See footnote *73° North*, p213

97. *Red Sky in the Morning*, p75

98. https://www.german-navy.de/kriegsmarine/articles/feature5.html

Chapter 28

99.　　https://www.german-navy.de/kriegsmarine/articles/feature5.html

100.　　https://www.german-navy.de/kriegsmarine/articles/feature5.html

101.　　https://www.german-navy.de/kriegsmarine/articles/feature5.html

Chapter 29

102.　　*Wartime Wanderings*, pp127-128

103.　　*Wartime Wanderings*, pp127-128

104.　　*73° North*, p249

105.　　Kerslake, Chapter 7–*Convoy JW51B*

106.　　*Wartime Wanderings*, p129

107.　　Private paper from the Bean family

108.　　Kerslake, Chapter 7–*Convoy JW51B*

109.　　Kerslake, Chapter 7–*Convoy JW51B*

110.　　Kerslake, Chapter 7–*Convoy JW51B*

111.　　Kerslake, Chapter 7–*Convoy JW51B*

Chapter 30

112.　　*Wartime Wanderings*, pp131-132

Chapter 31

113.　　*Red Sky in the Morning*, p97

114.　　https://www.wrecksite.eu/wreck.aspx?188704

Chapter 32

115.　　*Wartime Wanderings*, p135

116.　　*Wartime Wanderings*, pp135-136

Chapter 33

117.　　*Red Sky in the Morning*, p113

118.　　*Red Sky in the Morning*, p99

119.　　Melhuish, p59

120.　　Admiral Tovey in Foreword to *73° North*, pp11-13

Image List and Permissions

1	Churchill's Finest Hour Notes	Reproduced with permission of Curtis Brown, London, on behalf of The Estate of Winston S. Churchill © The Estate of Winston S. Churchill.
2	Lt Com. Ronald Weyman	Canadian Military History magazine
3	Bow damage to HMS *Achates*	Krígssavnið, War Museum, Faroe Islands
4	Survivors from mine explosion	Canadian Military History magazine
5	HMS *Achates* towed backwards	Krígssavnið, War Museum, Faroe Islands
6	Hedgehog anti-sub device	Alamy
7	24 pattern Hedgehog just fired	Alamy
8	HMS *Achates* after refit	Alamy
9	*Empire Lawrenc*e with CAM plane	Alamy
10	Ice field in Arctic	The Bean family collection
11	Heinkel on snow-covered airfield	Alamy
12	*Empire Purcell* on fire	Hartlepool Borough Council.
13	Chipping ice from ventilators and lockers	Alamy with colourisation
14	Convoy cargo being unloaded at Murmansk	Alamy
15	Lorry on quay Murmansk	Alamy
16	En route to rowing competition	The Bean family collection
17	Rowing competition, Murmansk.	The Bean family collection
18	Tirpitz German Battleship	Alamy
19	German reconnaissance of PQ17	Canadian Military History magazine

20	Lifeboats from American ship, *Carlton*.	Naval History and Heritage Command: Photo Section, Photo NH71305
21	Cargo ship in PQ17 sunk.	Naval History and Heritage Command: Photo Section, Photo NH71303
22	Commodore Melhuish	Arnold Melhuish
23	Wooden meeting hut, Loch Ewe	
24	Clearing deck of snow on HMS Scylla	Alamy with colourisation
25	Deck of *KG5* covered in snow in Arctic	Alamy with colourisation
26	Commander Robert St Vincent Sherbrooke	Wikipedia
27	Alex Macleod, Waternish	William Macleod, brother of Alex Macleod
28	David Macdonald 1st Day	David Macdonald family collection
29	David's last letter	David Macdonald family collection
30	Kenneth MacIver portrait	Iain MacIver family collection
31	Crew of HMS *Achates*	David Macdonald family collection
32	Short Sunderland on convoy duty	Alamy
33	Admiral Oscar Kummetz	Bundesarchiv Bild 183
34	*Admiral Hipp*er Recognition Drawing	Alamy
35	HMS *Scylla* using steam hoses to clear decks	Alamy with colourisation
36	HMS *Vansittart b*reaking the ice	Alamy with colourisation
37	*Admiral Hipper* Battleship Norway	Alamy
38	*Lützow* in Altenfjord	Albumwar2.com
39	*Admiral Hipper* from air with anti-torpedo net	Naval History and Heritage Command: Photo Section, Photo 110792
40	Three submarines in sub pen in Trondheim	Alamy
41	German U-boats outside sub pen in Trondheim	Alamy

42	Royal Navy destroyer laying down smoke	Alamy
43	Artist impression of Hipper firing	Naval & Heritage Command (Mr Jacoby): Photo Section, Photo NH61836
44	Hipper's 8" guns	Tony DiGiulan, Nav.com with colourisation
45	The Hipper firing on HMS *Glowworm*	Alamy with colourisation
46	Damaged Funnel and bridge area of HMS *Onslow*	Alamy
47	HMS Achates with radar cabin arrowed	Alamy
48	Box-lamp	Alamy
49	Rescue ship HMT *Northern Gem*	Alamy
50	Carley float	Alamy
51	George Drummond	2013 Russian Convoy Exhibition Loch Ewe. Provenance unknown.
52	Lieutenant Horace Aisthorpe	2013 Russian Convoy Exhibition Loch Ewe. Provenance unknown.
53	Aldis lamp	Alamy
54	Peyton Jones' letters	The Peyton Jones family collection
55	Appendix 1	The Peyton Jones family collection
56	Appendix 2	The Peyton Jones family collection
57	Appendix 3	David Macdonald family collection
58	Appendix 4	John MacIver family collection
59	Appendix 5	The Bean family collection
60	Appendix 6	From former owner of Aultbea Hotel, Loch Ewe

Maps and diagrams

Maps licensed from Adobe Stock

Textual information and detailing RG Maclean